CUBA'S ★CAR★ CULTURE

CELEBRATING THE ISLAND'S AUTOMOTIVE LOVE AFFAIR

TOM COTTER AND **BILL WARNER**

FOREWORD BY

SIR STIRLING MOSS

motorbooks

Quarto is the authority on a wide range of topics.

Quarto educates, entertains and enriches the lives of our readers—enthusiasts and lovers of hands-on living.

www.quartoknows.com

First published in 2016 by Motorbooks, an imprint of Quarto Publishing Group USA Inc., 400 First Avenue North, Suite 400, Minneapolis, MN 55401 USA. Telephone: (612) 344-8100 Fax: (612) 344-8692

quartoknows.com

Visit our blogs at quartoknows.com

Motorbooks titles are also available at discounts in bulk quantity for industrial or sales-promotional use. For details contact the Special Sales Manager at Quarto Publishing Group USA Inc., 400 First Avenue North, Suite 400, Minneapolis, MN 55401 USA.

10 9 8 7 6 5 4 3 2 1

ISBN: 978-0-7603-5026-3

Library of Congress Cataloging-in-Publication Data

Names: Cotter, Tom, 1954- author. | Warner, Bill, author.
Title: Cuba's car culture : celebrating the island's automotive love affair /
    Tom Cotter and Bill Warner ; foreword by Sir Stirling Moss.
Description: Minneapolis, MN, USA : Motorbooks, an imprint of Quarto
    Publishing Group USA, 2016. | Includes bibliographical references and index.
Identifiers: LCCN 2016015438 | ISBN 9780760350263 (hardbound)
Subjects: LCSH: Antique and classic cars--Cuba. | Cuba--Description and travel.
Classification: LCC TL33.C83 C68 2016 | DDC 629.222097291--dc23
LC record available at https://lccn.loc.gov/2016015438

Acquiring Editor: Zack Miller
Project Manager: Madeleine Vasaly
Art Director: Brad Springer
Cover Designer: Richard Aquan
Interior Design and Layout: Renato Stanisic

Front cover: *Ephraim Muller*
Back cover: *Roxana Gonzalez/Shutterstock*
Table of contents: *Jim Heimann Collection/Getty Images*
Acknowledgments: *Anne-Marie Weber/Getty Images*
Title page: *Patrik Bergström/Getty Images*
Front endpaper: *Historic Map Works LLC/Getty Images*
Back endpaper: *Universal Images Group/Getty Images*

Printed in China

This book is dedicated to the hard-working, ingenious, and proud Cuban motorists who have managed to keep their cars operating decades after their warranties expired.

....

ACKNOWLEDGMENTS

Thanks to Neil Rashba, Mildred Diaz (the Cuban travel guru!), Eduardo Mesejo Maestre, Joel Finn (*Caribbean Capers*), Richard Schweid (*Che's Chevrolet, Castro's Oldsmobile*), Dick Messer, Scott George, Ivan Celestrin, Kathleen Adelson (General Motors), the University of Miami Cuban Heritage Collection, and all the folks who gave us information whom we could only mention by their first names: Quico, Abel, Abe. And thank you to Motorbooks: Zack Miller, Madeleine Vasaly, and Brad Springer.

CONTENTS

FOREWORD

BY SIR STIRLING MOSS

It has been over fifty years since my last victory in the Cuban Grand Prix for sports cars. I drove in all three races, with victory in two of them—one in a Ferrari 335S and the last in the fabulous Maserati Tipo 61 for Camoradi USA (Casner Motor Racing Division). I've not been back to Cuba since then, although I was scheduled to return for Maserati a few years back, but the trip never materialized. The kidnapping of "El Maestro," Juan Manuel Fangio, in 1958 somewhat defined the direction the country was to go. In this book, Tom Cotter and Bill Warner have presented stories and photographs of the automotive culture that still lives in the hearts of the Cubans. The depth of enjoyment they were able to experience in essentially a police state is admirable, if not a little bit dangerous. Enjoy the stories and savor the dreams. The package will open soon, and Cuba will never be the same.

BELOW: Race winner Stirling Moss on the airport circuit en route to winning Cuba's last international race. *Collection of Bill Warner*
OPPOSITE: This 1955 poster rendering by Charlie Zito was used as the event poster for the 1957 Grand Prix. The Cuban Sporting Commission printed five thousand for distribution in the United States. *Collection of Bill Warner*

INTRODUCTION

TOM COTTER

I've always wanted to travel back in time rather than forward—perhaps it's because I'm more intrigued with history than the future. So in 2009, when my friend Bill Warner invited me to join him on an old car tour to Cuba to research the Cuban Grands Prix, I jumped at the offer to step back into the 1950s.

The country was amazing, and even though I don't agree with a political structure that put millions of citizens into poverty, I met many, many Cubans who were proud of their country and proud to be Cubans. During that trip, I fell in love with the people, the scenery, the architecture, the food, and the history. And, of course, the cars.

I decided that I wouldn't mind living in Cuba for a year. It would be an ideal locale to write a book, as Ernest Hemingway had discovered decades earlier.

Then, during the summer of 2015, Bill invited me to join him on another trip to the island nation. Of course I accepted. That's when we decided to write this book; I would do most of the writing, and Bill would handle all the photography.

Of all the books I've written, this one was the most difficult. You see, I don't speak Spanish, so all my interviews took at least twice as long because I had to go through translators. But I hope these words give you some idea about the state of the Cuban car culture.

We won't spend a lot of time on the politics of the trade embargo on these pages; numerous academic studies and other books already exist on that subject. So, unless it relates to automobiles, we'll avoid those topics. For the record, we don't think the embargo had as much impact as Cuba's failing economy. If the Cuban populace had the money, they could have bought whatever they needed from countries not participating in the US embargo.

Interestingly, while I was writing this book, I was also writing a book about a Route 66 road trip that I took around the same time. Both Cuba and Route 66 are stuck in the 1950s, and both offer visitors an opportunity to step back a half century in time. I encourage you to visit both, because both are a disappearing breed.

But visit Cuba first, because when they start building McDonald's restaurants and Home Depots, it'll be too late.

US-Cuba relations were changing rapidly as this book was being written, so it would not be surprising if relations were normalized by the time this book is sitting in your hands.

1

WELCOME TO CUBA: SET YOUR WATCH BACK FIFTY YEARS

OUR STEP BACK IN TIME DIDN'T OCCUR AS WE STEPPED ONTO CUBAN SOIL, BUT ACTUALLY BEFORE WE LEFT MIAMI. THE JET THAT WOULD TAKE US TO HAVANA, JUST OVER 200 MILES AWAY, WAS OWNED AND OPERATED BY HAVANA AIR BUT LIVERIED AS EASTERN AIR LINES. YOU REMEMBER—THE AIRLINE THAT WENT BANKRUPT TWENTY-FIVE YEARS AGO? DAVID NESSLEIN, CEO OF HAVANA AIR, ACQUIRED THE EASTERN NAME AND LOGO, AND NOW OPERATES "EASTERN" AS A CHARTER AIRLINE FLYING FROM MIAMI TO HAVANA AND BACK DAILY.

WE RECEIVED PERMISSION TO VISIT CUBA TO CONDUCT RESEARCH ABOUT THE COUNTRY'S AUTOMOTIVE HISTORY.

The prettiest cars, mostly convertibles, await tourists on the plaza outside the Parque Central hotel in central Havana.

Uber it's not—a 1952 Buick taxi prowls the back streets of Havana in search of a fare. This is likely a taxi for Cuban residents, since tourists prefer the shiny convertible cabs. *wellsie82/Getty Images*

Although we would have preferred to visit the island in January, February, or March—when the weather must resemble paradise—July, with its heat and humidity, was the only time that all three of our schedules were clear.

The reason we were going to Cuba was specifically to research this book. Our car-guy friend Wellington Morton had the week off and offered to accompany us on this trip.

We walked down the stairs of our Eastern jet, across the tarmac, and into the lobby of Havana's José Martí International Airport, where the scene in front of us could have been a movie set from a 1950s flick about a banana republic. Flights from around the world use the larger, more modern terminal across the runway, but flights from the United States are relegated to this smaller, antiquated, and rundown one. No doubt

ABOVE: We noticed this Ferrari decal on the fender of a Russian Lada. It is an accessory that even Cubans can afford!

BELOW RIGHT: The Parque Central is a European-style hotel that is located in the middle of Havana's business and tourist district. Taxis are parked out front to take you wherever you desire.

it's punishment for the embargo that the United States put in place in 1962 after Fidel Castro came into power. We'd soon discover that the worn-out airport was representative of the condition of just about everything else we'd see in the country.

Once we retrieved our luggage, which for no good reason took way too long (probably more punishment for Americans), we walked through the exit and toward the curb. We passed waving people who were probably seeing a family member from the United States for the first time in fifty years, taxi drivers holding crudely printed signs, and well-dressed tour operators ready to whisk away affluent vacationers to exotic resorts on the far ends of the island.

Then we saw the guards holding machine guns.

Once we made it through that crowd, we finally noticed what we'd come here to see: old cars that looked appropriate in front of the sixty-year-old airport terminal building we had just exited. There were pink Ford Thunderbirds, finned Cadillacs, Plymouth station wagons, red Chevy convertibles, mag wheels on nearly everything, and Ferrari stickers on vintage Ramblers.

Welcome to Cuba, the country that time forgot. The flight from Miami was just forty-five minutes, but that Eastern Air Lines jet had doubled as a time machine, bringing us and the rest of the passengers back in time more than half a century.

US banks? Nope.

US credit cards? Nope.

US-friendly ATMs? Personal checks? Cell phones? Nope, nope, nope.

We stayed in the wonderful Hotel Parque Central. It might not have been the most authentic hotel on the island, but both the air conditioning and the mojitos were cold.

(Though US cell phones don't currently work on the antiquated Cuban system, if you have a Cuban friend, they can buy a phone for you to use during your visit. If you don't have that friend to expedite the process, however, it could take you a few hours.)

Thankfully we took care of many of those incidentals before we left the States. And thankfully we had pockets full of American cash that could be exchanged at a rate of nearly one to one for Cuban convertible pesos (CUCs), the currency used for visitors to the island. We would trade our Yankee bucks for CUCs at a currency kiosk in the hotel for a 13 percent fee, but we'd also be able to purchase a great Cuban sandwich for just CUC$4 and the best mojito or piña colada we'd ever tasted for just CUC$5.

On the way to the hotel, we saw a couple hundred cars that could have been taken from the set of the early *Leave It to Beaver* television series. Initially, we got whiplash as we looked at every old car we passed. "Look, a Buick Roadmaster." "A Chrysler 300." "Look, there's a 1953 Ford Ranch Wagon." "Ooh, that's a sweet '57 Bel Air."

As we would soon discover, neck wrenching was not necessary; we would see many, many more vintage cars over the course of our stay.

Just a few blocks from the elegant Parque Central, this is a typical street scene. The 1958 Plymouth and 1956 Cadillac are parked next to once-elegant buildings, now in need of restoration.

2
CARS AND CASTRO'S REVOLUTION

C ARS PLAYED A MAJOR ROLE IN FIDEL CASTRO'S RISE TO POWER. IN RICHARD SCHWEID'S EXCELLENT BOOK *CHE'S CHEVROLET, FIDEL'S OLDSMOBILE*, HE DESCRIBES SOME OF THE VEHICLES THAT THE YOUNG CASTRO, HIS BROTHER RAÚL, ERNESTO "CHE" GUEVARA, AND OTHER KEY REVOLUTIONARY FIGURES USED BEFORE AND DURING THE ASSAULT. CASTRO WAXES ON NOSTALGICALLY IN HIS AUTOBIOGRAPHY, *FIDEL: MY EARLY YEARS*, ABOUT HIS 1950 CHEVY, WHICH SERVED HIM WELL IN HIS PREPARATIONS BEFORE THE ASSAULT.

LEFT: Despite the broken window, this tidy red 1952 Chevy sedan stands in sharp contrast to the building's weathered façade. *Dan Gair/Getty Images*

RIGHT: Fifty years later, Americans have long forgotten Castro's revolution, but Cubans live with the US embargo every day. Here a woman displays the flag of the revolution from her apartment window.

TIERRA DE INTERNACIONALISTAS

TOP: Cuban citizens are reminded daily of the revolution.

ABOVE: It's hard to escape images of the revolution wherever one travels throughout Cuba. This tank, along with other vehicles used during Castro's takeover, is on display at the Museum of the Revolution in Havana.

ABOVE RIGHT: Uninspiring apartment buildings like these are remnants of the three decades that the Soviet Union had a heavy influence in Cuba's economy. They are similar to buildings the Soviets built in Poland, Eastern Germany, and other former Eastern Bloc countries.

"I covered some 50,000 kilometers in a little car I had, a Chevrolet 50-315 [sic]," wrote Castro. "I bought it on credit; they were always taking it away from me."

Apparently the car had burned two days before the actual revolution began, but by then many of the cars used by his revolutionary army were rented. During the actual revolution, Castro drove a green 1959 Oldsmobile equipped with a V-8 engine, a Hydramatic transmission, and power steering. Younger brother Raúl used a 1951 Chevy as his transport during the time he and fellow revolutionaries were planning and executing their revolution.

Guevara's choice of wheels was a deep-green 1960 Chevy with a white top, powered by a 283-cubic-inch engine and a Powerglide automatic transmission. The car was apparently one of the last new models sold by Ambar Motors, Havana's major GM dealer, before shutting down as a result of the revolution. It is now on display at the Depósito del Automóvil car museum on Havana's waterfront. (There is no record of the whereabouts of Fidel Castro's Oldsmobile.)

One of Guevara's assistants appropriated a Jaguar from its wealthy owner who had fled to Florida during the revolution. Guevara roundly criticized him for driving a car that did not represent the people and gave the assistant—who loved the car—just two hours to return it.

ABOVE: One of the remnants of the Soviet era in Cuba is the occasional viewing of a Russian Chaika limousine, the staff car of choice for Russian political figures of the day.

LEFT: As Chaikas are not particularly attractive, it's obvious that Russian designers stole styling cues from some of America's most forgettable vehicles, especially Chrysler and Mercury.

ABOVE: Cuba's capitol building is nearly an exact replica of the United States Capitol building in Washington, D.C. The building has been maintained and remains one of Cuba's most beautiful.

RIGHT: The Statue of José Martí, father of Cuba's Independence from Spain, occupies the center of Parque Central in the historic district of Havana.

FAR RIGHT: Statues of American heroes, including this of President Abraham Lincoln, have been displayed in front of the capitol building for more than half a century.

JANUARY 1, 1959: THE DAY EVERYTHING CHANGED

Probably never imagining the impact his takeover would have on his country's industry, commerce, and infrastructure when he claimed himself leader of Cuba on New Year's Day, 1959, Fidel Alejandro Castro Ruz threw the country into an economic suspended animation that persists today.

The United States promptly responded to Castro's rise in power by placing an embargo on all trade relations with Cuba. This meant the United States was denied Cuban cigars, rum, and sugar, but Cuba was denied so much more. US-based companies—Coca-Cola, Frigidaire, Chevrolet, and hundreds of others—ceased doing business on the island, and that embargo was still in effect at the time of this writing.

ABOVE: A photo of the newly restored opera house taken from the roof of the Hotel Parque Central. One by one, many of Havana's significant buildings are being restored.

BELOW: Not quite Concours: these three vehicles—Plymouth, Ford, and Rambler, all in rough condition—seem to have been painted with the same brush.

RIGHT: Ladies in colorful Cuban garb will pose with a cigar for you for 3 CUCs.

OPPOSITE PAGE: Dick Messer, former director of the Petersen Automotive Museum in Los Angeles, enjoys the company of one of these famous "cigar ladies" of Havana.

ABOVE: It's not uncommon to see collapsed buildings throughout Havana. The entire country's infrastructure needs a half century's worth of maintenance and repair. It is said that one building collapses every third day.

RIGHT: Oxen-drawn carts are still in use throughout the Cuban countryside, mostly to haul produce to market or water to irrigate the fields.

Once part of a beautiful city, these buildings are now overcrowded and falling down. Some tenants even raise chickens and pigs on their balconies.

One by one, Ford, General Motors, Chrysler, and Rambler dealership owners shuttered their storefronts and escaped to America, South America, and beyond. For the first few months, or maybe even a year or two, life continued pretty much unchanged for the Cuban citizens who were forced to remain on the island. But as their cars started to break down, the supply of spare parts started to rapidly dry up.

It was like the world's cruelest joke: Cubans were driving thousands of American cars just 90 miles from Key West, Florida, yet they could source no American parts to keep them in good running order. Instead, motorists were forced to adapt parts made in Russia and Czechoslovakia, many of which were designed for trucks and tractors, slowly converting their cars to automotive Frankensteins.

Over time, the car owners of Cuba have become, by necessity, possibly the most competent mechanics on the planet.

This 1951 Buick convertible from the NostalgiCar taxi company takes a tourist past one of Havana's many crumbling buildings. *Holly Wilmeth/Getty Images*

3
COLORFUL YA★NK TANKS

I N *CHE'S CHEVROLET, CASTRO'S OLDSMOBILE,* RICHARD SCHWEID ESTIMATES THAT TODAY MORE THAN SIXTY THOUSAND PRE-1960 AMERICAN CARS PROWL THE STREETS OF CUBA, MOST OF THEM IN THE CONGESTED CITIES OF HAVANA AND SANTIAGO DE CUBA. OF THOSE, ROUGHLY HALF ARE FROM THE 1950s, 25 PERCENT ARE FROM THE 1940s, AND 25 PERCENT ARE FROM THE 1930s.

IF YOU WERE TO STAND ON A BUSY STREET CORNER IN THE CENTER OF HAVANA NEAR THE HOTEL PARQUE CENTRAL, YOU WOULD SEE DOZENS AND DOZENS OF COLORFUL AMERICAN CARS, PARKED ALONG THE CURB,

Owners of vintage cars in Cuba maintain and clean them regularly, but given the choice, they would gladly trade their sixty-year-old relics for modern, more economical cars that have luxuries such as air conditioning.

waiting for taxi clients, or vying for a spot in the moving parking lot that embraces this center city from sunrise to sunset. Interspersed between the old American iron is an odd mix of 1970s Russian-built Ladas (retooled Italian Fiat 131 sedans), new Chinese Geelys (which resemble late-model Cadillacs and Chevys), and the occasional Soviet-era Volga, Wartburg, or Škoda. Once in a while, you might see a late-model Mercedes-Benz or Audi negotiating the many potholes that exist on Cuban streets; these, we were told, belong to diplomats or non-American corporate executives, possibly from one of the oil companies that do business on the island.

LEFT: In what could almost be a scene from nearly any American city half a century ago, the photo of these American cars waiting at a traffic light was taken in 2015. *wellsie82/Getty Images*

BELOW: Originally, a large eagle facing America sat atop these twin columns—the Monument to the Victims of the USS *Maine*—but Castro had it removed. The famous Hotel Nacional de Cuba is in the background.

ABOVE: When have you seen another one of these? This 1955 Cadillac has been modified into a station-wagon configuration by some enterprising Cuban.

RIGHT: This bright yellow Chrysler taxi, which appears to be a 1956 model, offers its patrons a spacious interior. Is it still Hemi powered? We never caught up with the driver to find out.

CARS ARE CUBA'S BRAND

If you've seen a magazine article, news segment, or Travel Channel TV show about Cuba during the past decade, chances are the first image was that of colorful old American cars. Those cars have become the country's brand, and it's probably the first topic of conversation you are likely to hear when you mention Cuba to friends, family, and especially car guys.

We hear the same mantra all the time from our car-enthusiast friends: "When relations between the United States and Cuba open up, I'm going to go down there and buy a bunch of those old cars, then bring them back to the States and sell them for a fortune!" We hate to burst bubbles, but even if it were legal to export a car from Cuba—which it's currently not—a few days on the island will quickly change most car enthusiasts' opinions.

In the States, car guys have an expression to describe cars that look worse the closer they get: 30-footers. From 30 feet away, the car looks great, but its flaws become more apparent with every step closer.

In Cuba, we coined the phrase 100-yarders!

The colorful Cuban cars you see on the Discovery Channel, or in *Traveler* magazine, don't tell the full story. When you read about " impeccably restored classic American cars," don't believe a word of it.

continued on page 40

This 1953 Studebaker coupe looks pretty cool with its faux Minilite wheels. The Raymond Loewy–designed car is beautiful, regardless of what country in which it resides.

This 1950 Plymouth seems to have the famous Malecón highway to itself as the wind and the waves whip up the ocean on the right. *danm/ Getty Images*

ABOVE: This 1957 Chevy 210 two-door hardtop looks as though some details and a paint job are all it needs to be presentable, even in the States.

LEFT: A combination of two hood mascots adorns this Cuban beauty.

continued from page 37

In all fairness, the cars that are restored to a high level by Cuban standards would rank as No. 4 in the United States, according to *Sports Car Market*'s valuation criteria. But 99.9 percent of the American cars on the road here are finished to a far lower level, ranking five and below. They have been patched and bandaged together for decades. The term "restored" is academic. These cars are nostalgic—old and still running, but that's about it. Very few truly restored cars exist on the island, mostly due to lack of money, talent, and/or materials.

Think of the car sitting in your driveway. When it's new, everything is tight and works flawlessly. But as the new-car smell dissipates and more miles accumulate on the odometer, your car will start to develop squeaks and rattles, and parts will begin to fail. By the time it's five or six or seven years old, you'll probably start thinking about trading it in for a new model.

Now compare that five- or six- or seven-year-old car to the average Cuban's fifty- or sixty-or seventy-year-old cars. We even saw some eighty-year-olds—Model As and 1935 Fords—that were still operating on a daily basis. Compound that age with incredibly rough roads, poor gas quality, and an almost complete absence of correct spare parts, and you'll begin to appreciate just how ingenious the Cubans are.

From 100 yards, the cars of Cuba can easily be identified as Fords and Chevys and Pontiacs. But

ABOVE: There are many dogs roaming loose in Cuba, but this one is obviously more fashionable than most.

BELOW: How can you tell that a legendary Rocket 88 no longer resides under the hood of this 1953 Oldsmobile? The black smoke pouring out of the tailpipe means it's probably a diesel tractor motor.

ABOVE: The rough-around-the-edges condition of this Buick is representative of most of the vintage American cars plying the streets of Cuba.

BELOW: When was the last time you saw one of these? This 1958 Edsel Pacer convertible is rare even in America, but one this nice in Cuba is truly a treasure. The owner, a photographer, uses the car primarily for weddings.

the closer you get, the more subtle styling changes become visible. Over time, the cars have become an automotive "stew," with parts from one year or brand of car adapted to fit on another.

It's not unusual to see a 1951 Chevy with a 1955 Chevy grille. Or VW taillights adapted to a Buick. Sometimes these swapped parts look totally plastered on, just installed to get the car back on the road. But often, local craftsmen actually sculpt the new pieces onto cars in a very convincing

manner. Cubans are proud people, and even though most of them are very poor, they try to keep their cars looking respectable.

Trim items such as grilles and bumpers are taken from other cars when they exist, but local craftsmen have also become quite adept at beating metal into the same approximate shape as the original item. Sometimes trim pieces are wrapped in tin foil to give the illusion of being chrome. It's not perfect, but in a pinch, it works.

This beautiful 1959 Buick convertible was as nice as any we've seen in the States. It was, of course, in livery service in the historic district.

This 1958 Buick four-door hardtop appeared flawless and is in use as a taxi (see the sign on the dash).

4

THE MYTH ★ OF THE ★ ROMANCE

THE CUBAN PEOPLE ARE SO TIRED OF THESE OLD PIECES-OF-SHIT CARS," SAID OUR TRANSLATOR, ABE. "THEY RUN ON NOTHING! IF THEY EVER HAVE A CHANCE TO BUY A NEW CAR, THEY WILL!"

SO MANY TV SHOWS AND MAGAZINE STORIES HAVE BEEN WRITTEN ABOUT THE LOVE AFFAIRS THAT CUBAN OWNERS HAVE WITH THEIR CARS, AND HOW METICULOUSLY RESTORED AND CARED FOR THEY ARE.

NOPE.

ABE VOCALIZES WHAT NEARLY EVERY CUBAN FEELS, BUT CANNOT SAY, FOR FEAR OF RETALIATION. THE TRUTH IS THAT THEY HOLD NO ROMANCE IN THE OLD CARS THEY DRIVE; THAT ROMANCE EXISTS ONLY FOR THE TOURISTS WHO HAVE NOT SEEN SIMILAR CARS FOR HALF A CENTURY.

A 1958 Chevy is parked on a stone-paved street in downtown Havana. *Merten Snijders/ Getty Images*

Cubans repair and use these old cars because that's all they can do—there are no alternatives. It's necessity, not a love affair.

These cars provide incomes to thousands of residents who might not have another way to scrape together a living in this failing economy. "Once the Russian economy collapsed, and we stopped receiving support from the Soviets, we started to receive tourists again," said Abe.

"Now Cubans look forward to better relations between our two countries, so they are all trying to get their cars in better condition."

CUBA'S BLACK MARKET

During our first trip to Cuba back in 2009, we were naïve and actually believed that folks survived on the equivalent of just $5 in US dollars a week. While that may be true in some cases, probably for farmers and those living in the rural parts of the country, that rule does not apply to everyone.

At CUC$20 per month—the government stipend each Cuban citizen receives regardless of whether

Obviously, some owners have the time and the financial wherewithal to keep their cars in better-than-average condition. This 1951 Pontiac is one of the best cars we saw.

Chevrolets are still very popular in Cuba, as witnessed by this lineup. Left to right are a 1954, a 1952, and a 1950, all in livery service by the train station.

they are a doctor or a street sweeper—a citizen cannot save CUC$30,000 in their lifetime to buy a used car. According to Abe, twenty bucks a month is not enough to pay the power bill and buy groceries.

In addition to the stipend, each Cuban citizen receives a small amount of chicken, sugar, and a few other necessities. But residents have found often ingenious ways to supplement their meager salaries.

It's ironic that one of the Earth's last strong-holds of Communism is also a breeding ground for capitalism and entrepreneurship. So many people have "side deals" that there is actually a healthy underground economy—and for some, a thriving one. Cubans often turn their dining rooms into makeshift restaurants that offer tourists the chance to taste authentic, home-cooked island food. Those handy with tools will do auto repairs literally in the street, performing everything from brake jobs to engine rebuilds on the side of the

road. And there are plenty of English-speaking Cubans who will make their services available as translators and tour guides for tourists.

"In Cuba, people pretend to work, and the government pretends to pay," is what we were told by one tour guide. He also gave us this bit of wisdom: "Cuba is the only country where

continued on page 53

NON-WOOD WOODIES

It's odd to see a 1940s-vintage Ford station wagon without any wood at all, but with an all-steel body. In the States, Ford woody wagons were built with wood bodies from the Model T era all the way to 1951, but somehow Cuba became the recipient of coach-built steel station wagons before the States did. Where did those cars come from? Were they built in Cuba or in the United States? Nobody was able to give us answers.

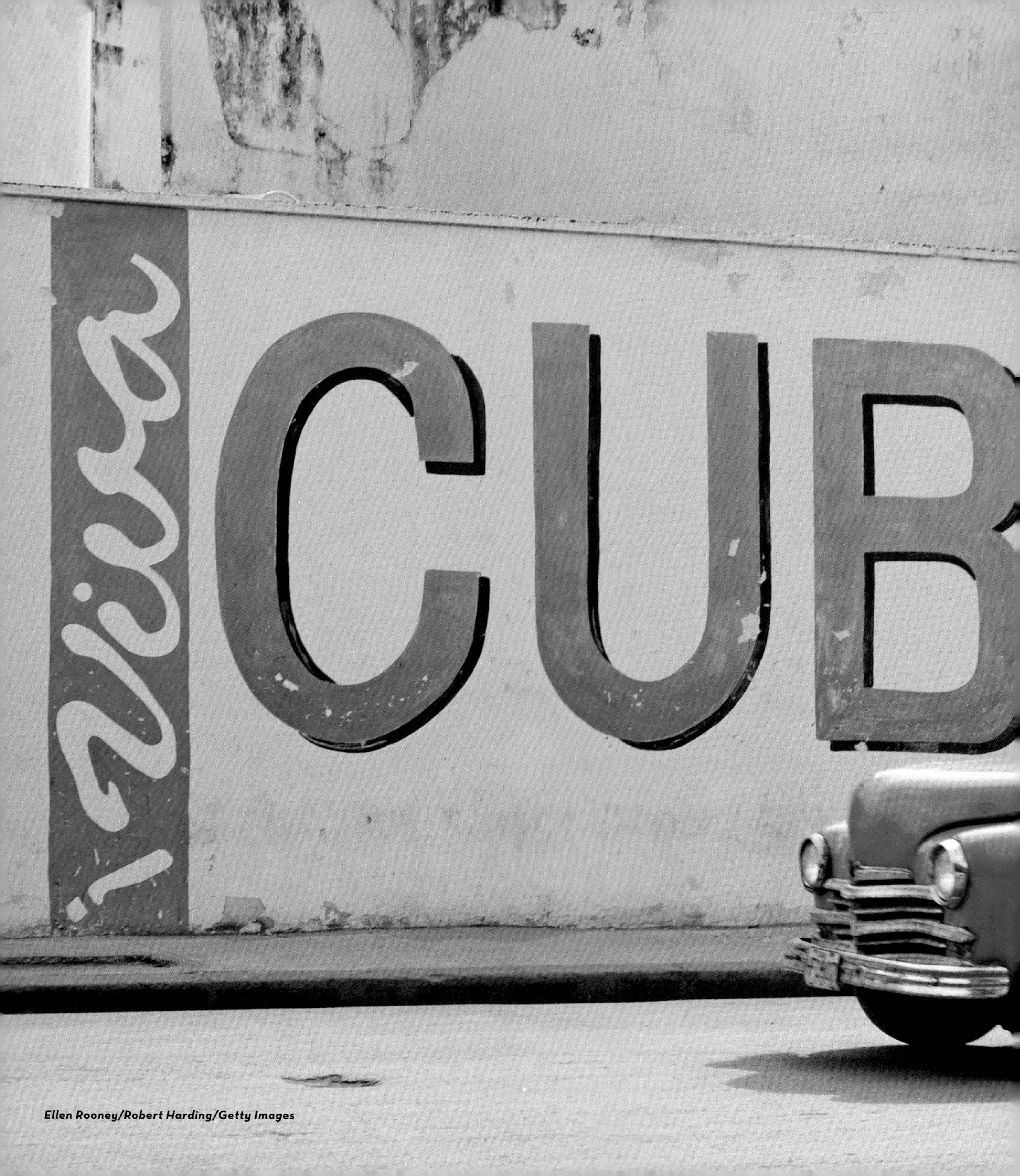

Ellen Rooney/Robert Harding/Getty Images

TRAVELING TO AND AROUND CUBA

The first time I visited Cuba, in 2009, I was pulled aside in the airport customs area for a lengthy "routine" check. While my four traveling companions patiently waited in the crowded baggage claim area, I was asked many questions about the purpose of my visit to Cuba.

After about thirty minutes, I was released. I suppose a person is chosen at random from every flight, and this time I was the lucky guinea pig. When I walked outside the airport, I noticed armed guards with machine guns stationed at the corners of the terminal. Good thing I didn't try to bolt while I was being questioned.

—TOM COTTER

continued from page 49

you can live without working, but you can't live if you work."

In automotive terms, this underground economy explains how a rough but running 1958 Chevy four-door sedan could be *se vende* (for sale) with an asking price equivalent to roughly US$35,000. That same car in the States could be purchased for one-third that amount. And the stateside car would certainly be in better condition, with more original parts still intact.

It's all about supply and demand; fewer cars on the market mean consumers must pay top dollar to purchase one. And purchasing a car is only possible because of the flourishing black market.

It appears that the Cuban government simply turns a blind eye to this parallel economy. The personal incomes of many everyday Cubans are likely several times larger than they admit.

OPPOSITE PAGE: A real "late model," the 1960 Ford in the foreground must be one of the last American cars to be shipped to Cuba before the embargo was put into effect.

RIGHT: The face of Che Guevara festoons a building at the Plaza de la Revolución. *Albin Hillert/Shutterstock*

5
ISLAND ★CARS:★
A HUNDRED-YEAR HISTORY

CARS HAVE BEEN AN ESSENTIAL PART OF CUBAN CULTURE SINCE BEFORE THE LAST CENTURY. EARLY ENTREPRENEURS WHO SAW PROMISE IN THE SELF-PROPELLED, FOUR-WHEELED CONTRAPTION IMAGINED MAKING RICHES FROM THEIR IMPORTS. BUT, MORE OFTEN THAN NOT, THOSE ENTREPRENEURS PUT THE CART BEFORE THE HORSE—OR, IN THIS CASE, THE CAR BEFORE THE ROAD.

MANY WHO ATTEMPTED TO IMPORT CARS INTO THE COUNTRY WENT BROKE BECAUSE OF POOR TIMING: CUBANS NEEDED VEHICLES, BUT THEIR "ROADS" WERE

In the 1950s, GM in general, and Chevy in particular, sold more cars in Cuba than any other brand. Tri-Five Chevys, like this 1955, are still some of the most popular cars on Cuban roads today. *Courtesy General Motors Archives.*

1 CYL. CADILLAC, 1904-05

© The GROGAN PHOTO COMPANY *Danville. Ill.*

ABOVE: Cadillacs have been imported to Cuba since the company's earliest days. One-cylinder models like this 1904–1905 model once traveled on Cuba's crude dirt, gravel, and limited paved roads. *Library of Congress*

BELOW: Because of their extremely low prices, Model T Fords eventually became the best-selling automobile in Cuba. *Library of Congress*

4 CYL. MODEL T
FORD, 1908

We found this original Ford in a garage in Santiago de Cuba. The owner lives in Miami, but laws prevent him from removing his vintage racer from Cuba.

in such a horrid state that they could only be driven short distances. Often they were nothing more than narrow, muddy goat paths.

The first recorded car to enter Cuba was called a Parisienne, a French vehicle that arrived in Havana in 1898. The two-horsepower vehicle was capable of a top speed of 7 miles per hour and cost US$1,000, the equivalent of more than $28,000 in 2016, when adjusted for inflation. Because of its high price and the limited areas in which prospective customers could drive it, it made for a tough sell to Cuban citizens.

The second car appeared a year later, in 1899, and was a Rochet-Schneider. Also built in France, the five-seater car was priced at US$4,000 (equivalent to more than $100,000 in 2016), but when compared to the Parisienne, it was a virtual

speed demon: the eight-horsepower engine had a top speed of 12 miles per hour, nearly double that of its predecessor. Later that year, four bus-type vehicles were sent to Havana in the hopes of establishing regular commuter routes.

Today we drive faster than 12 miles per hour in an average parking lot, but in Cuba at the turn of the last century, that speed was faster than a horse pulling a wagon. And cars, unlike horses, only needed to be fed when they were used, so the attraction of self-propelled vehicles was obvious.

In 1900, another Parisienne was shipped to Havana. Later that year, two Locomobiles were shipped from New York. The first car to arrive in Cuba's second-largest city, Santiago de Cuba, came in 1902. It was another Locomobile and was powered by a steam engine.

All these vehicles were owned by businessmen who hoped to capitalize on the new four-wheeled phenomenon that was sweeping other modern societies. But with the horrible condition of the roads—well, horse paths and trails—they had the right idea, but too soon.

Initially, American brands such as Oldsmobile and White had a hard time getting a foothold in the Cuban market because wealthy families bought European brands such as De Dion Bouton, Panhard et Levassor, and the already mentioned Rochet-Schneider. In 1905, Cuban businessman Germán López secured the franchises for both Fiat and Locomobile, and Cuba's first car dealership opened. López built a shop large enough to work on six cars at once, the first of its kind in the country.

The following year, 1906, the first vehicle accident resulting in a fatality occurred in Cuba. The driver of the car had apparently been drinking and hit a pedestrian. That accident, in part, resulted in the institution of a Cuba's first drivers' licenses.

By 1913, there were more than four thousand motorized vehicles on the island. And while the most popular brands were still built in Europe, American brands were beginning to make headway. Packards, Chevrolets, Cadillacs, and Dodges were appearing on the streets more often, but it took Ford Motor Company to begin pushing the European brands out of the limelight.

The Model T eventually became Cuba's best-selling car, spurred on by its simple design and low price. While most European cars were selling for thousands of dollars, a 1913 Model T sold for just US$550. The next year the price dropped to $400, and by 1916 customers could purchase a brand new Model T for just $365! Suddenly cars were not just for the wealthy but within the grasp of the middle class as well.

In 1914, Ernesto Carricaburu, a one-time chauffer and race driver, bought ten Model T Fords and began Cuba's first recorded taxi service. In a letter notifying his managers in Dearborn, Michigan, of the purchase, Ford foreign manager E. C. Sherman brought his US colleagues up to speed on Cuba's economic scene: "Cuba's population is 2.5 million people, and 80% of those are poor," he wrote. "It is estimated that 50% of the population cannot read or write. There are 2,000 miles of roads in Cuba that can be driven year round." He went on to say that much of the island transportation was still by means of mule or horse, "because the trails are too narrow for an ox-cart, let alone an automobile."

Cuba, where ten thousand cars were plying the roads, was certainly the largest Latin American automobile market in 1917. At the time, Cuba was the ninth-largest Latin American country in population, but between the government and individuals, the country was responsible for buying more cars than much larger nations, such as Argentina, Brazil, and Mexico.

By 1922, of the 5,117 cars imported to Cuba, 4,722 were American made. Travel within the cities of Havana, Santiago de Cuba, and a couple other urban areas was getting better, but most people who traveled from one end of Cuba to another traveled by sea. The roads along the 750-mile island were still in horrid condition.

Ford outsold all other American brands until the mid-1930s. In 1936, Chevrolet exported 1,076 cars to Cuba and Ford shipped 1,069, a difference

More Cadillacs per capita were sold in Cuba than in any other country, including the United States, before the embargo. It is suspected that many of those were sold to mobsters who ran gambling and prostitution operations on the island.

of only 7 cars. But GM cars increasingly dominated car sales in Cuba until the 1959 embargo.

In 1946, 16,258 cars were registered to individuals in Cuba, but only six years later, in 1952, that number jumped to more than 77,000. In that year, of the 14,725 automobiles imported to Cuba, 95 percent were built in the United States. That translated to more than US$25 million worth of sales to dealerships at wholesale prices. Added to that were 7,800 trucks sold on the island, adding another $13 million to the bottom line.

"Most of our dealers have been making a lot of money," wrote C. M. Dolittle, general manager of Havana's Ford branch, to R. I. Roberge, export manager in Michigan.

6

INTERNATIONAL ★ AUTO ★ RACING

THE FIRST AUTO RACE IN CUBA WAS HELD IN HAVANA IN 1903, HOSTED BY THE HAVANA AUTOMOBILE CLUB. FIVE CARS WERE ENTERED, INCLUDING AT LEAST ONE GERMAN MERCEDES AND A FRENCH DARRACQ. DÁMASO LAINÉ, DRIVING THE DARRACQ, WON WITH HIS WIFE RIDING IN THE PASSENGER SEAT.

THE COUNTRY'S SECOND RACE WAS IN 1905 AND WAS SANCTIONED BY THE INTERNATIONAL ASSOCIATION OF AUTOMOBILE RACING. IT INCLUDED DRIVERS FROM AROUND THE WORLD WHO COMPETED ON A 99-MILE COURSE. ERNESTO CARRICABURU, THE SAME MAN WHO WOULD BRING TEN MODEL TS TO CUBA TO BEGIN A TAXI BUSINESS A DECADE LATER, WON IN A MERCEDES WITH

Juan Manuel Fangio (in a Maserati 330S) leads Peter Collins (in a Ferrari 500TR) through Havana's streets. *Collection of Bill Warner*

TOP: Cuba's first horseracing track, Parque Oriental, also known as the Hippodrome, began promoting auto racing events in 1916. This photo is from a 1918 event. *University of Miami, Cuban Heritage Collection*

ABOVE: Driver Marcelino Amador and teammates in their Cadillac-powered race cars at the Parque Oriental race in 1918. *University of Miami, Cuban Heritage Collection*

In 1925, five drivers competed in a speed record attempt to drive 531 miles, starting in Santiago de Cuba and ending in Havana. It took the winner just over nine days to go the distance, as drivers battled torrential rains and flooding along the route. Newspapers called the drivers heroes. A year later, four drivers competed in a similar race, taking just under three days to go the same distance.

STOCK CARS

Most of the cars that competed in early Cuban auto races were cut-down, open-wheel affairs with either one or two seats. These were early predecessors of today's Formula One and Indy race cars. But occasionally races were held for "stock-bodied" cars.

Roberto Vegas was considered one of Cuba's top drivers from the 1930s until the 1950s. His most successful mount? Not a lightweight coupe or roadster, but a 1928 seven-passenger Lincoln sedan. The behemoth vehicle was supposedly built for a Chicago gangster and had bulletproof glass and armor plating installed. Somehow the car wound up in Cuba in 1930 and was used by then-president Gerardo Machado. Later, the car sat behind a Lincoln dealership, then was sold to a junkyard for scrap.

Vegas, seeing potential in the giant, stripped it of its heavy glass and armor plating and turned it into a race car. He souped up the original V-12 engine, painted the black sedan yellow, and began winning races against cars that were seemingly much lighter and faster. In one stretch of seventeen races, Vegas won ten in the gargantuan Lincoln. He often started dead last, because he volunteered to use his car to "push-start" the race cars of other competitors whose engines refused to fire.

an average speed of 53 miles per hour. Carricaburu's speed was a world record at the time. He also set a record for driving from Havana to Matanzas, about 68 miles apart, in just one hour and twelve minutes.

Auto racing became more popular, and in 1907, events were held on the La Sierra horseracing track in Havana instead of on public roads. As in the modern era, races were held in order to market vehicles to consumers—or as we call it today, "win on Sunday, sell on Monday." The more cars that were sold, the more races were held.

MIDGETS AND "BIG CARS"

Just prior to World War II, much of the racing taking place in Cuba actually originated in the Northeast United States. The owners of Midget race cars—smaller-scale open-wheel racers, most often powered by V-8 60 Ford flathead engines but occasionally by twin-cam Offenhauser power plants—were encouraged to come to Havana and race their cars during the winter months in 1939 and 1940.

A hotbed of Midget racing, Freeport Raceway on Long Island advertised that drivers could race in Cuba three nights per week during the months of February, March, and April. Not a bad proposition for snow-bound racers who were counting the days until Northeast races began again.

Havana's races often were staged in the Stadium Tropical, but occasionally on beaches as well. Most drivers traveled to Cuba from New York and Tampa, Florida, but occasionally drivers traveled from New Jersey, Pennsylvania, and even Canada. Even if they didn't win, drivers considered it an all-expenses-paid vacation.

Stock-car racing was popular in Cuba for decades. Here, in a race on downtown Havana streets, are a 1956 Ford Victoria and a 1957 Chevy sports cedan. *University of Miami, Cuban Heritage Collection*

POST–WORLD WAR II, CUBA'S RACING ERA

New York racing promotors Jake Kedenburg and Duke Donaldson were encouraged to begin bringing American drivers to Cuba after the war. The site of most prewar races, La Tropical stadium, was not available because of a heavy baseball schedule, so races were conducted at Autódromo Nacional, a half-mile track that was suitable for sprint cars, stock cars, midgets, and motorcycles.

American drivers were guaranteed US$50 per week as appearance money if they raced against Cuban drivers in Havana. Unlike in prewar years, the US drivers mostly rented rides in Cuban-owned cars, thereby keeping their travel expenses to a minimum. Some of the standout American drivers who ventured south included Buzz Barton, Speed Wynn, and Pete Folse.

The six-race series was considered a success, with the Cuban drivers showing that they had become as talented as their American competitors.

Interestingly, one of the most renowned American drivers of the era, Tommy Hinnershitz, and his number one sprint car were featured on the cover of the race program for the December 16, 1951, Autódromo Nacional races, but there is no record of Hinnershitz ever racing in Cuba.

ROAD RACING ATTRACTS TOURISTS

After controversial dictator Fulgencio Batista's coup made him the leader of Cuba in 1952, he

Tall and narrow, a Jaguar XK120 speeds along the long Malecón main straightaway. The outside wall separates the race cars from the water below. *Collection of Bill Warner*

sought to expand Cuba's presence in all forms of sport. He built soccer and baseball fields, running tracks, swimming pools, and gymnasiums throughout the country, allowing citizens to use these facilities at no charge.

Seeing how the popularity of road races such as the Bahamas Speed Week and events in Argentina and Sebring, Florida, were attracting tourists, Batista put plans in place to host international races in Cuba. The Cuban Sporting Commission (CSC) met with officials of the Fédération Internationale de l'Automobile (FIA) in Europe to schedule a race after the Caracas and Bahamas races but before Argentina and Sebring.

A date of February 25, 1955, was chosen, and a series of sports and stock car races were held through the streets of old Havana and on the scenic Malecón, a wide, elevated highway above the ocean in Havana. A roughly 3½-mile circuit was designed to run counterclockwise along a mostly straight route with a few left-hand turns.

But the FIA was concerned about Cuba hosting an internationally sanctioned Grand Prix, having never hosted a race before, so they rejected Cuba's request. Because of the horrific accident that occurred at the 1955 Le Mans race in June—when a Mercedes-Benz race car vaulted into the grandstands, killing eighty-three spectators—the organization was concerned about driver and spectator safety, given the proposed course's tall curbing and potentially high speeds.

After the FIA denied request after request from Cuba to host a non-championship Grand Prix, a World Sports Car Manufacturers Championship race, and a 1,000-kilometer endurance event, the governing organization finally approved a 500-kilometer

RIGHT: Longtime journalist and automotive PR guy Bob Fendell was issued these (misspelled) credentials so he could cover the 1957 Cuban Grand Prix for the *New York World-Telegram.* Collection of Bill Warner

non-championship race for sports and stock cars to be held on February 25, 1957.

Prior to the FIA-sanctioned events, Cuba had hosted its own series of events, called the Cuban National Races—which included the Pinar del Rio–Havana rally, among others—from 1954 until 1956. The long-distance rallies were driven on public roads, some as long as 187 miles. They attracted mostly Cuban drivers in cars ranging from MG TDs and Jaguars to Lincoln and Buick sedans.

THE GRAND PRIX BECOMES REALITY: THE 1957 CUBAN GRAND PRIX

Cuban sports officials had the foresight to realize that nobody in that country had the connections to attract top racing talent to their first Grand Prix. So three "agents" were hired to help convince the top teams to participate. The Automobile Club of Milan (Italy) was in charge of attracting teams from Europe; driver Juan Manuel Fangio's manager, Marcello Giambertone, had the responsibility to recruit South American teams; and US Ferrari importer Luigi Chinetti was in charge of Ferrari entries.

The organizers agreed that Fangio needed to be an entrant. Besides being considered a racing god in South America after winning multiple Grand Prix titles for both Mercedes and Ferrari, his entry would add legitimacy to the entire event. Fangio had left the Ferrari team at the end of the 1956 season, so he would be competing in a Maserati 300S in Havana. Some of the other well-known drivers committed to the race were Stirling Moss (Maserati 300S), Carroll Shelby (Ferrari 410 Sport), Phil Hill (Ferrari 860 Monza) and Masten Gregory (Ferrari 500 TR).

Cuban organizers decided that only World Sports Car Manufacturers Championship cars would be invited, meaning no production-based vehicles—such as the Mercedes-Benz 300SL—could participate. Also, no American-powered Ferraris or Maseratis could enter. (American engines transplanted into Italian sports cars was a popular modification in the United States at the time.) The organizers were only interested in genuine Ferraris and Maseratis competing. Further, race cars under two liters were not invited, meaning that Porsches and OSCAs could not compete, because it was feared the smaller-horsepower cars would have an extreme disadvantage in the high-speed Malecón circuit.

In the days leading up to race day, most of the drivers made laps around the circuit in their street cars to become familiar with the layout. On the Friday before the race, practice sessions began with drivers in their race cars. Some drivers complained of some nasty bumps and rough

OPPOSITE: Poster design for the 1958 Grand Prix. *Motorbooks collection*

STARTING GRID FOR THE 1957 CUBAN GRAND PRIX

1.	Juan Manuel Fangio	Maserati 300S
2.	Alfonso de Portago	Ferrari 860 Monza
3.	Phil Hill	Ferrari 860 Monza
4.	Harry Schell	Maserati 300S
5.	Carroll Shelby	Ferrari 410 Sport
6.	Stirling Moss	Maserati 200S
7.	Eugenio Castellotti	Ferrari 860 Monza
8.	Alfonso Gómez Mena	Jaguar D Type
9.	Jean Lucas	Ferrari 121LM
10.	Olivier Gendebien	Ferrari 250 TR
11.	Masten Gregory	Ferrari 250 TR
12.	Piero Drogo	Ferrari 250 TR
13.	Ottavio Guarducci	Ferrari Mondial
14.	Piero Carini	Ferrari 375+
15.	Manuel Perez de la Mesa	Maserati 200S
16.	Peter Collins	Ferrari 250 TR
17.	Howard Hively	Ferrari 375 Plus
18.	Alessandro de Tomaso	Maserati 150/200S

patches brought on by the high heat drawing the oil up from the pavement. Additionally, because water flowed beneath the elevated road surface, sections of the pavement continually became undermined. Road crews worked feverishly to keep the road surface in good shape for the race.

The FIA required that the Automobile Club of Milan be contracted to provide communications, race control, and logistics for the Cuban organizers because of the host's lack of experience.

When race day finally arrived, Cuban fans were thrilled to see the high-powered cars at speed. Fangio started on the pole, followed by Alfonso de Portago, Phil Hill, and Harry Schell. At the standing

ABOVE: Olivier Gendebien in the Ferrari 500TR owned by Bill Helburn. He qualified ninth and finished fifth. Helburn was a terrible driver, so Gendebien did all the work. *Collection of Bill Warner*

RIGHT: After leading much of the race, Alfonso de Portago's Ferrari 860 Monza finished third. In the process, he turned the race's fastest lap. *Collection of Bill Warner*

start, Hill stalled on the grid, which left his car momentarily powerless and a dangerous obstacle for the other racers to navigate around. Carroll Shelby's very powerful Ferrari launched into the lead for one lap, but the ill-handling car spun at the first turn on lap two, and he fell back to fourth. Moss dropped out early when his oil pressure dropped to zero because of a ruptured oil line in his Maserati.

Drivers in the race were recording lap times in the 2.4-minute range, about the same as Fangio's pole qualifying lap.

By the middle of the race, de Portago was leading with Fangio, the only other car on the lead lap, close behind, probably waiting for the leader to

continued on page 74

RIGHT: Carroll Shelby muscles the Ferrari 410 Sport to a second-place finish behind the Maestro, Juan Fangio. *Collection of Bill Warner*

Marquis Alfonso de Portago awaits the start of the 1957 Grand Prix, delayed by rain. *Collection of Bill Warner*

continued from page 70

pit before attempting to take the lead. Fangio had started with a heavy load of fuel and was biding his time and conserving his brakes before making his move. Shelby was in third, one lap down, followed by Castellotti, Gendebien, and Gregory.

De Portago came into the pits on lap sixty-nine of the ninety-lap race with fuel pressure problems; his fuel line had cracked, and his car suddenly slowed to a crawl. As mechanics feverishly worked on his car, de Portago screamed, cursed, and banged on the car for them to get the job done until Luigi Chinetti pleaded with him to stop his tirade.

As de Portago sat in the pits for more than five minutes, Fangio, who had inherited the lead, passed the pits twice. When de Portago finally reentered the race, nearly three laps down to Fangio and two to Shelby, the PA announcer had the Cuban crowd in a frenzy cheering on the Spanish driver. De Portago passed Shelby and Fangio once, but the race was too short to make up any more laps on the leader. During his frenzy to make up for his lengthy pit stop, de Portago recorded the race's fastest lap of 2 minutes, 1.1 seconds.

Fangio held on to the lead and won the 500-kilometer race in 3 hours, 11 minutes for an average speed of 98.2 miles per hour. Shelby finished second and de Portago was third.

President Batista was on hand to award Fangio a gold trophy. However, on his way back to his mansion after the race, the leader's limo was caught in traffic caused by people leaving the event. Fans shouted for Batista to help find them jobs. His police escort began to beat the spectators and fired gunshots into the air to scatter the crowd.

It was an unfortunate ending to an otherwise wonderful day.

After the award ceremony, de Portago complained loudly that he had been robbed—that he should have won the race. The crowd started to cheer for him, at which point race winner Fangio came over and put his winner's wreath around de Portago's neck. The crowd went wild and de Portago became embarrassed at all the attention.

Of the seventeen starters, only eight cars were still running at the race's conclusion.

1958 CUBAN GRAND PRIX: A RACE OF CALAMITY

An FIA rules change for 1958 put a maximum engine displacement at three liters for that year's race, which meant the big-engined Ferraris and Maseratis were relegated out of the series.

Another notable difference was that three drivers who had competed in the inaugural Cuban Grand Prix the year before—Eugenio Castellotti, Alfonso de Portago, and Piero Carini—had died during that season.

After Cuba had proven itself by hosting a successful Grand Prix, the FIA granted the country

1957 CUBAN GRAND PRIX RACE RESULTS

1. Juan Manuel Fangio
2. Carroll Shelby
3. Alfonso de Portago
4. Peter Collins
5. Olivier Gendebien
6. Alfonso Gómez Mena
7. Piero Drogo
8. Masten Gregory

DID NOT FINISH
Phil Hill
Howard Hively
Stirling Moss
Harry Schell
Eugenio Castellotti
Jean Lucas
Piero Carini
Alessandro de Tomaso
Ottavio Guarducci

the rights to conduct a second race in 1958. The length would be the same (ninety laps), as would the prize money (US$1,500 for first place, $1,000 for second, and $500 for third, fourth, and fifth—plus another $500 for winning the pole position). A growing concern for race organizers was the increasing unrest caused by the Communists, who were upset that the inaugural Grand Prix had been a success in all regards. The Communists complained that the races siphoned money away from social programs, such as finding employment for unemployed farm workers, and warned an accident like the Le Mans Mercedes-Benz crash

This unidentified beauty poses against Wolfgang Von Trips's Ferrari 315S prior to the start of the 1958 Grand Prix. Perhaps she rubbed on some good luck, because Von Trips finished fourth. *Collection of Bill Warner*

could easily happen in Cuba. Suddenly politicians began talking about a ban on auto racing on Cuban roads. Many also feared that the Communists would booby-trap or otherwise disrupt the race activities.

Juan Fangio won his fifth and final world championship by the end of 1957 and announced his retirement from full-time racing. He decided, at forty-seven years old, to enter only a couple of races in 1958, then leave the sport for good. He would only compete in races that meant a lot

to him during his farewell tour, and Cuba was certainly on that list.

Fangio received $5,000 appearance money and agreed to race a Maserati owned by American architect and car collector Temple Buell in the Cuban event.

As the race neared, rumors and media speculation that the Communists would attempt to disrupt the race began circulating. There were whispers that bombs would be placed around the circuit and that tacks and oily liquids would be put in fast corners.

De Portago on the outside in the No. 12 Ferrari 410 races wheel-to-wheel against Juan Fangio in the No. 2 Maserati in the turn at the end of the long Malecón straightaway, 1957. Collection of Bill Warner

Communists passed out leaflets warning spectators to stay indoors; foreign drivers were assigned bodyguards, and there was a heavy police and military presence around the circuit.

Cubans knew that Communists were often bearded men, so anyone with facial hair was viewed suspiciously. In an embarrassing episode, Finnish driver Jo Bonnier was arrested because he sported a beard and held for several hours of questioning before being released.

Separately, the overall health of Cuba's racing administration was put to the test during pre-race activities, and it was in shambles. Nobody seemed to be in charge of driver registration, and workers were afraid to make decisions. Because Cuba had hosted a successful event twelve months earlier, the FIA rescinded the requirement to contract the Automobile Club of Milan to operate all aspects of race control. The Cuban organizers thought this would be an ideal way to save money, but the foolhardiness of that decision was becoming more apparent every day.

There was also concern from the start about the race's infrastructure. There was no radio communication around the circuit, and few ambulances and medical personnel were present.

When practice began, drivers complained of some amazingly slippery turns. It was suspected that some of the stock car races that were held earlier in the day may have oiled down the track. During practice, cars were sliding off the track and slamming curbs, and without proper radio communication and flags to warn the drivers, it kept happening over and over.

A local driver, Diego Veguilla, died when his car's steering broke at high speed along the Malecón straightaway. His car flipped and hit a light pole, and Veguilla was thrown from his car into the pole and died instantly. The car's gas tank broke from the car and caught on fire, yet because communications were so bad, emergency personnel weren't notified of the severity of the accident. Few timing and scoring people were experienced, and stopwatches were in short supply. As a result, lap times were estimated. A professional time-keeper from Sebring arrived with a state-of-the-art stopwatch setup, which featured a split-time function, but halfway through Sunday morning's practice, the timing unit fell from its shelf onto concrete 10 feet below and was destroyed.

Despite all of this, Fangio was recorded fastest with a 1 minute, 59 second lap, decisively faster than one year earlier. Moss went out late in qualifying with fresh tires and minimum fuel and cut a lap of 1 minute, 58 seconds. All other competitors were 2 minutes or more.

BELOW: Peter Collins, in Howard Hively's Ferrari 500TR, finished fourth overall. *Collection of Bill Warner*

FANGIO KIDNAPPED!

Revolutionaries continued to make threats of disrupting the Grand Prix, but they had done that before and nothing much ever came of them. This time, though, they were serious, and it would shake the auto racing world to its core.

The great Juan Manuel Fangio of Argentina preferred the quiet ambiance of the Hotel Lincoln—at the time a first-class property that featured the Three Wise Monkeys bar and intimate rooms—to the more lavish Hotel Nacional, where most drivers stayed. The Lincoln was built in 1926 and featured 134 rooms spread over nine stories. Fangio preferred room number 810, and it was reserved for him whenever he visited Havana.

At 8:45 p.m. the evening before the Grand Prix, Fangio was standing in the crowded lobby with several associates from the Maserati team when a stranger approached holding a Colt .45 pistol. Two other armed gunmen were guarding the lobby doors. According to fellow driver Alessandro de Tomaso's report to the police after the incident, this is what happened:

"Which one of you is Fangio?" the stranger asked.

"I am," said the world champion driver. "What do you want?"

"Come with me," the gunman said. "I'm from the Twenty-Sixth of July Movement [Castro's revolution]. Don't resist and you won't be hurt."

The gunman pushed his pistol into Fangio's side, and the two began making their way toward the exit. The entire kidnapping took less than one minute to complete.

Within minutes of Fangio's removal, the Hotel Lincoln lobby was filled with police and army personnel. The revolutionaries almost immediately contacted the media, notifying them that they had kidnapped the great race driver in protest against the Cuban government using public funds to promote the race while many Cubans were unemployed. This was a charge that local sports officials denied. Members of the 26th of July Movement claimed they kidnaped Fangio in order to gain international attention and to embarrass the Batista government.

Police and soldiers searched houses and buildings belonging to known sympathizers but never turned up a lead. There had been no word about Fangio's whereabouts for hours, and friends and journalists waited in the Hotel Lincoln lobby for updates on the kidnapping.

Organizers decided to conduct the race even without Fangio's presence.

TOP: Juan Manuel Fangio in the No. 2 Maserati during practice for the Cuba Grand Prix on Saturday, the day before the race. That night he would be kidnapped from his hotel. *Collection of Bill Warner*

STARTING GRID FOR THE 1958 CUBAN GRAND PRIX

1.	Stirling Moss	Ferrari 335S
2.	Masten GregoryFerrari	410 Sport
3.	Carroll Shelby	Maserati 450S
4.	Jean Behra	Maserati 300S
5.	Phil Hill	Ferrari 335S
6.	Ed Crawford	Ferrari 290MM
7.	Wolfgang von Trips	Ferrari 315S
8.	Paul O'Shea	Ferrari 290MM
9.	Piero Drogo	Ferrari 250TR
10.	Roberto Mieres	Porsche 550 Spyder
11.	Francisco Godia Sales	Maserati 300S
12.	Harry Schell	Maserati 200S
13.	Bruce Kessler	Ferrari 500TRC
14.	Jo Bonnier	Maserati 200S
15.	Boris (Bob) Said	Ferrari 500TRC
16.	Jim Kimberly	Maserati 450S
17.	Maurice Trintignant	Maserati 450S
18.	Giorgio Scarlatti	Maserati 200S
19.	Fritz d'Orey	Porsche 550 Spyder
20.	Ulf Norinder	Porsche 550 Spyder
21.	Cesare Perdisa	Maserati 300S
22.	Porfirio Rubirosa	Ferrari 500TRC
23.	Chet Flynn	Ferrari 500TRC
24.	Jorge Galtes	Ferrari 500TRC
25.	Manuel Perez de la Mesa	Ferrari 500 TRC
26.	Armando Garcia Cifuentes	Ferrari 500TRC
27.	Luigi Piotti	OSCA 1500

Race activities on the morning of February 24, 1958, began with the Cuban National Races for sports and stock cars. Cars such as Edsels, Studebakers, and Dodges competed in the stock car class, with Porsches and Mercedes 300SLs entered in various sports car classes.

Before the race, the pit and paddock areas were in turmoil, with scores of race fans disrupting drivers and mechanics making last-minute adjustments.

Race control was in complete chaos. The organizers had only two stopwatches before one fell onto the concrete and was stepped on. One of the two experienced timers had to leave for the United States, and a small, rag-tag group of inexperienced volunteers offered to help.

Communication around the circuit was almost nonexistent, and attending journalists described the scene as unrestrained bedlam.

With no sign of Fangio, driver Maurice Trintignant was offered the pole-qualifying car to race, but he would start from the fifth row.

Finally, after a confusing two-hour delay in the race start, the ninety-lap Grand Prix of Cuba took the green at 3:20 p.m. As a result of the delay spent idling in the heat, some cars overheated and others fouled spark plugs. The air was filled with smoke and unburned fuel as the front rows took off down the Malecón.

Masten Gregory shot ahead, followed by Stirling Moss and Phil Hill.

Several cars dropped oil around the circuit, and without any means of communication, no oil flags were displayed. The field slowed down as cautious drivers feared wrecking their cars.

On lap six, Armando Garcia Cifuentes lost control at a high-speed corner near the American Embassy, jumped the curb, and plowed into a group of spectators. Six spectators were killed and at least forty others were injured.

A red flag (to stop the race) was displayed, but because race control was out of sight, personnel could only guess that something was wrong on the other end of the track. Finally Phil Hill and Bob

Fangio on his way to victory in the 1957 Cuban GP. *Collection of Bill Warner*

SAFE AND SOUND

After the race, the Argentine ambassador to Cuba, Adm. Raúl Lynch, received a phone call telling him Fangio could be retrieved at a certain address. Lynch thought it was a prank call until the kidnappers put Fangio himself on the phone; the ambassador picked him up and brought him back to his residence.

Soon the media was alerted that Fangio was released and unharmed. Fangio said that his kidnappers had treated him like gentlemen, and were kind and courteous to him throughout the ordeal. He said he was moved first to a home near the Hotel Lincoln, then to a second, and finally a third home. While he was being transported, they asked the race driver to lie on the floor of the car in case gunfire erupted. He was held in a luxurious home, served breakfast in bed, and given a hot bath and dinner. He was also given a radio so he could listen to the races.

Fangio received his $5,000 appearance money from the race organizers even though he did not compete.

Said stopped at race control to inform them of what had happened. Gregory and Moss passed the accident, with leader Gregory slowing down and Moss taking the lead under the red flag.

The race lasted just six laps and thirteen minutes.

Moss was declared the winner, with Gregory in second. Gregory was upset because Moss had passed him under a red flag, which was usually not legal, but Moss reminded him that under international racing rules, a red flag could only be displayed at the start-finish line. The two men decided to split the first- and second-place prize money equally, each receiving $2,250, which seemed to satisfy both parties.

Carroll Shelby finished third, followed by Wolfgang von Trips and Harry Schell.

1960 CUBAN GRAND PRIX: CUBA'S LAST INTERNATIONAL RACE

Communist revolutionaries continued to try to convince Cuban citizens that they would be better off supporting their movement than Batista's right-wing dictatorship. Finally, on New Year's Day, 1959, Batista fled to the Dominican Republic, taking an estimated US$500 million in gold reserves with him.

Castro had won, but the Cuban economy was in shambles and getting worse by the day as foreign investment ground to a halt.

Despite the 1958 Grand Prix debacle, road racing continued for Cuban drivers in sports and stock cars at La Cayuga airport in San Antonio de los Baños and in the Marianao section of Havana in

1958 GRAND PRIX RESULTS

1. **Stirling Moss**
2. **Masten Gregory**
3. **Carroll Shelby**
4. **Wolfgang von Trips**
5. **Harry Schell**
6. **Jo Bonnier**
7. **Jean Behra**
8. **Ed Crawford**
9. **Paul O'Shea**
10. **Giorgio Scarlatti**
11. **Maurice Trintignant**
12. **Piero Drogo**
13. **Bruce Kessler**
14. **Bob Said**
15. **Jim Kimberly**
16. **Fritz d'Orey**
17. **Ulf Norinder**
18. **Phil Hill**
19. **Jorge Galtes**
20. **Francisco Godia Sales**
21. **Manuel Perez de la Mesa**
22. **Porfirio Rubirosa**
23. **Chet Flynn**
24. **Luigi Piotti**
25. **Roberto Mieres**
26. **Cesare Perdisa**
27. **Armando Garcia Cifuentes**

1958 and 1959. However, these races were poorly organized and attended, and because they were held on an active airport runway, they were halted any time a plane approached for a landing.

No Grand Prix was considered in 1959. But West Palm Beach racing organizer Ken Coleman approached the Castro regime about the possibility of hosting another race in Cuba as a way to spur tourism, which had declined rapidly after the Communist takeover. Castro's government was anxious to show that the country was still a viable tourist destination and supported the idea. The race was scheduled for February 28, 1960.

Coleman and his team determined that to improve spectator and driver safety, the Malecón was no longer a viable circuit and a new venue needed to be found. After an exhaustive search, a 3.1-mile circuit at Camp Liberty was chosen. The camp, outside of Havana, was formerly known as La Cayuga, a World War II–era US airbase that was named by its designers after the lake in New York where several of

them had grown up. The course would use some runways and some airport access roads, a few of which ran along the Havana Country Club. Spectator safety was paramount in the minds of the organizers, so retaining fences were erected with plenty of run-off area between the course and spectator areas.

The race was to be sixty-five laps in length, about 202 miles.

The FIA was leery about granting the Cuban Grand Prix an international sanction because of the disastrous 1958 race. Not surprisingly, they required assurances that an adequate communications system, with trained flagmen and corner workers, be secured before that sanction would be granted.

One of the preliminary races during the 1960 Havana Speed Week was for Formula Juniors. The rapid, lightweight cars were considered a steppingstone to Formula One. *Collection of Bill Warner*

Giacomo Russo, No. 42, drove his Stanguellini Formula Junior to seventh and second place in the weekend's two races, to finish third in the aggregate. Henri Grandsire in the No. 12 Stanguellini had problems, with only a last-place finish in one race. *Collection of Bill Warner*

Stirling Moss and Pedro Rodriguez would be paid US$5,000 each in appearance monies, and an all-star cast of other internationally known drivers was expected to participate as well.

In the twenty-four months since Cuba had last hosted an international race, much had changed in the sports car racing world. Maserati and Aston Martin no longer fielded factory teams, and Ferrari was not inclined to sell modern race cars to private teams. Porsche was eager to sell cars, but they could only dominate a race like this if there were many corners, not on the high-speed straights of the airport circuit.

A week before the Grand Prix, a Formula Junior race was held for cars that were considered a steppingstone to Grand Prix race cars. Not many American teams attended because Stanguellini

importer Briggs Cunningham was protesting the Cuban event over the Castro government taking control of a Cunningham-owned business in Cuba. Most entries came from South America, Italy, and France. Ken Coleman wrote to the FIA at the conclusion of the Junior race, informing the sanctioning body of his dissatisfaction with the race's management and asking that it be rectified.

On Wednesday of Havana Speed Week, sandwiched between the Formula Junior race on one weekend and concluding with the Grand Prix the next, a GT race was held for production-based cars such as the Mercedes 300SL and Corvette. Jim Jeffords in a Corvette was the class of the field, running on a lap of his own. Second-place Alfonso Gomez Mena finished more than one minute behind Jeffords in his Ferrari.

ABOVE: Odd Bedfellows: a Gemini-brand Formula Junior racecar shares the paddock with a machine-gun-toting military vehicle during the 1960 Grand Prix. *Collection of Bill Warner*

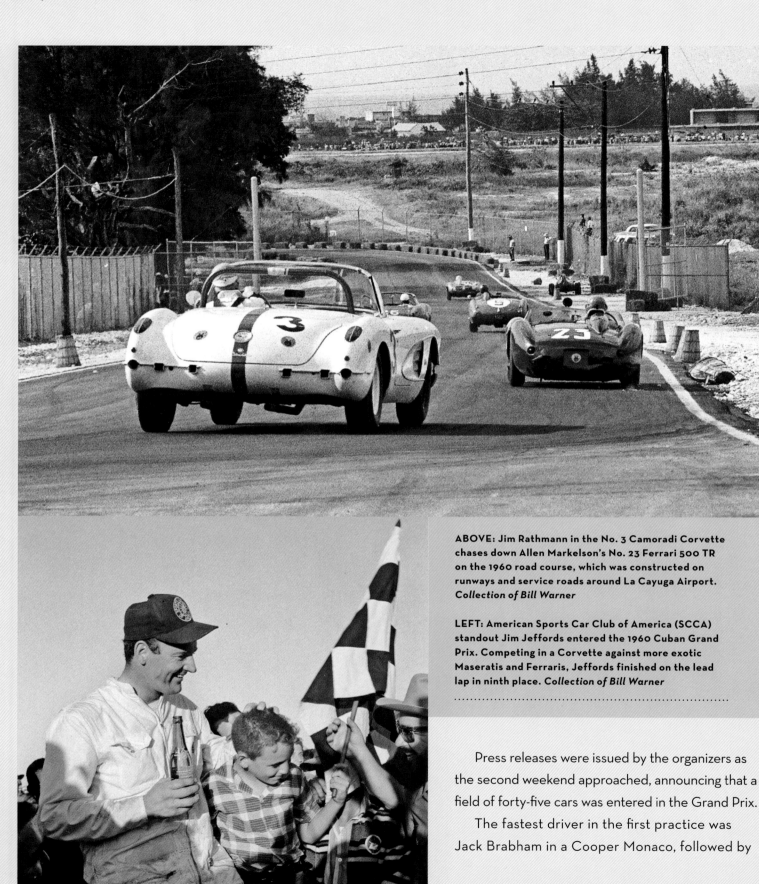

ABOVE: Jim Rathmann in the No. 3 Camoradi Corvette chases down Allen Markelson's No. 23 Ferrari 500 TR on the 1960 road course, which was constructed on runways and service roads around La Cayuga Airport. *Collection of Bill Warner*

LEFT: American Sports Car Club of America (SCCA) standout Jim Jeffords entered the 1960 Cuban Grand Prix. Competing in a Corvette against more exotic Maseratis and Ferraris, Jeffords finished on the lead lap in ninth place. *Collection of Bill Warner*

Press releases were issued by the organizers as the second weekend approached, announcing that a field of forty-five cars was entered in the Grand Prix. The fastest driver in the first practice was Jack Brabham in a Cooper Monaco, followed by

Jack Brabham installed a larger fuel tank in his Cooper Monaco, so the required spare tire had to be moved and secured in the passenger compartment. *Collection of Bill Warner*

George Constantine, also in a Cooper Monaco, and Pedro Rodriguez in a Ferrari. During the second practice, Stirling Moss recorded the fastest lap in a Camoradi USA Maserati Tipo 61, four seconds faster than Brabham.

During what appeared to be an otherwise faultless racing week, driver Ettore Chimeri crashed his Ferrari into a cyclone wire fence during practice after the car fishtailed, likely due

to faulty brakes. It tumbled over the fence and down a 150-foot embankment. Chimeri died on the scene.

Just one hour before the start of the Grand Prix on Sunday, race organizers informed competitors that their race would be shortened from sixty-five laps to fifty laps in order to accommodate a race for Cuban stock cars afterward. The order had come from Fidel

ABOVE: Maurice Trintignant's Maserati leads George Constantine's Cooper Monaco. *Collection of Bill Warner*

BELOW RIGHT: Masten Gregory in contemplation before buckling himself into his Porsche RSK. *Collection of Bill Warner*

Castro himself, and promoter Coleman reluctantly obliged. The Grand Prix race would now be just 155 miles as opposed to the original 202 miles. Records are unclear as to how many drivers actually started the Grand Prix; just before the start of the event, forty-four drivers were said to be ready to take the green flag, but afterwards, that number was reduced to forty-one starters, then to thirty-eight.

The race started as advertised at 3:00 p.m., when the drivers were given the signal to sprint across the track in a Le Mans–style start. It is estimated that between seventy thousand and one hundred thousand fans attended that hot, sunny day.

Moss was first across the track, jumping into his Maserati and sprinting off. Masten Gregory was not so lucky; as he jumped into his Porsche, one of his legs went between the steering wheel spokes and became jammed. It took almost forty-five seconds for Gregory to extricate his leg from the steering wheel and get under way; some say that it took so long because he was laughing so hard at his clumsiness. Other drivers having issues included Indy ace Rodger Ward, whose Ferrari wouldn't

start, and Eddie Sachs, whose Chevy-powered special flooded its carburetor.

Moss led from the start and was as much as forty-five seconds ahead of Rodriguez's Ferrari when he slowed down to a ten-second lead, partly because his seat mount had broken but partly to add some excitement to the race. He won the race with Pedro Rodriguez in second, the only two drivers to go the full fifty-lap distance. The third- and fourth-place

continued on page 92

Porsche RSK drivers Fritz d'Orey (No. 37) and Huschke von Hanstein try to chase down Stirling Moss's Maserati in the far distance. *Collection of Bill Warner*

Mexican standout Ricardo Rodriguez kneels next to his Porsche RSK prior to the race's start, seemingly installing a decal. Rodriguez did not finish due to clutch problems. *Collection of Bill Warner*

1960 GRAND PRIX RESULTS

1.	Stirling Moss	Maserati Tipo 61
2.	Pedro Rodriguez	Ferrari TR59
3.	Masten Gregory	Porsche RSK
4.	Huschke von Hanstein	Porsche RSK
5.	Colin Davis	Cooper-Maserati
6.	Maurice Trintignant	Maserati 300S
7.	Jo Bonnier	Porsche RSK
8.	Fritz d'Orey	Porsche RSK
9.	Jim Jeffords	Chevrolet Corvette
10.	George Constantine	Cooper Monaco
11.	Alfonso Gomez Mena	Ferrari 250 GT
12.	Francisco Godia Sales	OSCA 1500
13.	Jean Bonnet	Porsche RSK
14.	Rodger Ward/Dan Gurney	Ferrari 250 TR
15.	Ada Pace	OSCA 1500
16.	Teodoro Zecolli	OSCA 1500
17.	Johnny Cuevas	Porsche Carrera
18.	Fausto Gonzalez de Chavez	Jaguar XKSS
19.	Larry de Richelieu	Lotus 11
20.	Freddie Brandt	Maserati 200S
21.	Jim Rathmann	Chevrolet Corvette
22.	Marcelino Fayen	Ferrari 250 GT

DID NOT FINISH

Gabriel Riano	Porsche 550 Spyder
Allen Markelson	Ferrari 500TR
Loyal Katskee	Maserati Tipo 61
Eddie Sachs	Sadler Nissonger Special
Gino Munaron	Maserati 200S
Harry Schell	Maserati 300S
Carroll Shelby	Porsche 550 Spyder
Jack Brabham	Cooper Monaco
Ray Hixon	SHE Special
Dan Gurney	Maserati 200S
Ricardo Rodriguez	Porsche RSK
Ulf Norinder	Porsche RSK
Armando D'Ambroggio	Porsche RSK

ABOVE: Dan Gurney (left) and Stirling Moss, both early in their racing careers, seem to be discussing strategy prior to the start of the Grand Prix. *Collection of Bill Warner*

continued from page 89

finishers were Masten Gregory and Huschke van Heinstein, respectively, both in Porsche RSKs.

American Dan Gurney, whose Maserati's differential failed, sat in the pits until the last lap, when he sputtered around the circuit to take the checkered flag. But because he failed to complete the minimum twenty-five laps, his finish was disqualified.

CHECKERED FLAG

The 1960 race was seen as a success by the organizers and the fans. In fact, promoter Coleman and his associates suggested that a similar event be conducted the following year. But the Castro government thought otherwise.

A sport that had been part of Cuba's history since 1903—and that had brought drivers, teams, and tourists from around the world—was suddenly viewed as "frivolous and had no social value" by the new government. Racing would continue to be enjoyed in other parts of the world, but the checkered flag that fell on March 2, 1960, ended international racing in Cuba forever.

Rodger Ward in the Ferrari 250 TR he shared with a young Dan Gurney to finish fourteenth overall in the 1960 GP. *Collection of Bill Warner*

Stirling Moss and Maserati team chief mechanic Guerino Bertocchi taking a victory lap after Moss won the Grand Prix. *Collection of Bill Warner*

ABOVE: Stirling Moss in his Maserati gets a wave-by from Fausto Gonzalez de Chavez in a Jaguar XKSS. *Collection of Bill Warner*

BELOW: Huschke van Heinstein finished fourth overall in the Porsche RSK. *Collection of Bill Warner*

RACING TODAY

There is organized go-kart racing in Cuba on a purpose-built, paved track that may or may not have been built by the Catholic Church (we never could get confirmation one way or the other). And there is outlaw drag racing that happens on occasion on little-used roads. These events are hard to learn about, and they apparently happen on an irregular basis.

But the motorsport event that occurs annually and legally is the annual road rally, a 70-mile loop through Havana for nearly seventy cars, motorcycles, and even a four-wheel drive truck. Like a major automotive event in the United States, this rally has sponsors, such as Castrol. We were lucky enough to be in the country the same weekend as the rally, so we went to the start and met many of the excited participants.

TOP: Friend Dick Messer, who joined us on our 2009 trip, inspects an Italian-made Tony Kart at the Cuban karting facility. If nobody had been looking, Messer would have jumped in and taken a few laps.

ABOVE: This racer has his kart's tail hanging out as he clips a tight apex around a karting course about 15 miles from downtown Havana.

ABOVE: Road rallying around the world is primarily for sports cars. But in Cuba, there just are not enough sports cars, so a 1955 Chevy four-door gets the green flag for Cuba's largest motorsport event, a 70-kilometer road rally.

LEFT: Never seen a 1958 Cadillac four-door convertible? That's probably because Cadillac never manufactured one. But somebody in Cuba fabricated one and entered it in the rally.

A rare car anywhere in the world, this Triumph Vitesse convertible is a six-cylinder version of the four-cylinder Herald. This beauty doubles as a taxi.

7

LEFTOVER CLASSICS

★

BEFORE THE "TRIUMPH OF THE REVOLUTION," A TERM SOME LOYAL CUBANS PROUDLY REPEAT WHEN DISCUSSING FIDEL CASTRO'S RISE TO POWER, THERE WAS HUGE WEALTH ON THE ISLAND.

PRIOR TO CASTRO, CUBA'S LEADER WAS THE ONE-TIME CUBAN ARMY SERGEANT FULGENCIO BATISTA. IT WAS WELL KNOWN THAT HIS ADMINISTRATION WAS CORRUPT, WITH HIS CRONIES BECOMING VERY WEALTHY, WHILE MOST CUBANS LIVED IN SEVERE POVERTY. CUBA'S ECONOMY WAS BOOMING, BUT SO WERE GAMBLING, PROSTITUTION, AND OTHER ILLEGAL ACTIVITIES. MANY OF THOSE PROSPERING IN THE COUNTRY HAD TIES TO THE MAFIA THROUGH AMERICAN CASINO OWNER MEYER LANSKY.

THE JESUIT-EDUCATED FORMER LAW STUDENT FIDEL CASTRO LED A REVOLUTION THAT ULTIMATELY OVERTHREW THE BATISTA REGIME. WHEN BATISTA AND HIS HENCHMEN

A red 1953 Chevrolet Bel Air convertible sporting modern alloy wheels basks in the streetlights of Havana's historic district.

For such a poor nation, it is amazing how many Cadillacs can be seen driving the roads of Cuba. It gives tourists an idea of just how much wealth there once was on the island.

hopped on airplanes and flew off to South America and Florida, Castro found himself the leader of the island nation. Batista's supporters left behind many assets, including real estate, businesses, and expensive automobiles.

Those automobiles have since become the subject of fact, speculation, and folklore. We were lucky enough to meet owners of some interesting cars, who were as passionate about their vintage automobiles as any American enthusiast.

Please Note: In describing these cars, we use the word "classic" rather loosely. The Classic Car Club of America defines a classic car as from an "exclusive list that includes only specific important marques built largely between 1925 and 1948." Think Duesenberg, Bugatti, or Pierce-Arrow.

In this book, we use the word "classic" to describe the thousands of standard Fords and Chevys that are still running around the streets of Cuba. It's a word of convenience, mostly to describe the romance of Cuba's vintage cars.

WORLD'S LARGEST CADILLAC MARKET

In the 1950s, money was so plentiful on the island that more Cadillacs were sold per capita in Cuba than anyplace else on earth. And since many of Batista's followers owned Caddys, some of the cars seen on the road today may have a direct lineage to the controversial leader's regime.

"WE ALL LIVE IN A FLAT-BLACK LIMOUSINE . . ."

One Cadillac that has not seen road miles recently, however, is the 1958 Cadillac submarine car created by renowned Cuban artist and sculptor Esterio Segura. Esterio lives in a sprawling suburban villa that was built in 1924. His flat-black Cadillac is on display in his front yard, surrounded by a wrought-iron fence.

He told us the car is mechanically all original except for a Russian carburetor. It started out as a limousine, but he fabricated the rear body with sheet metal over a tubular-shaped structure, complete with portholes and a propeller.

"My first submarine car was built out of a Nash Cross Country, "said Esterio, whose artwork—which often includes submarine and airplane themes—has been displayed at galleries around the world. "I was going to build a submarine car out of my 1957 Cadillac Fleetwood, but it was in such good condition that I decided to buy this 1958 instead, which had been sitting for thirty years. This one was not so nice."

Esterio is not shy about converting large American vehicles into pieces of art.

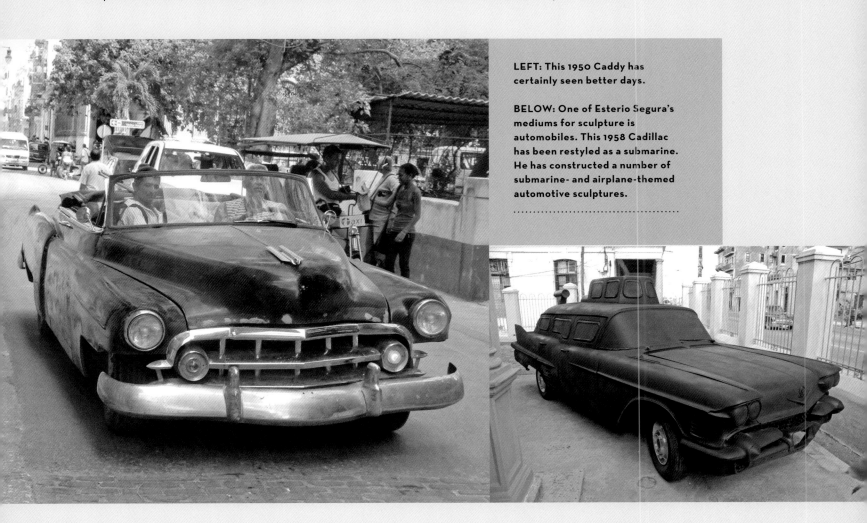

LEFT: This 1950 Caddy has certainly seen better days.

BELOW: One of Esterio Segura's mediums for sculpture is automobiles. This 1958 Cadillac has been restyled as a submarine. He has constructed a number of submarine- and airplane-themed automotive sculptures.

"My second automotive sculpture was a 1954 Chrysler limousine, which I converted into an airplane," he said. "While the car was being displayed at a gallery in Barcelona, it was damaged, so I had it shipped back to Cuba. I am rebuilding it now."

He is currently building another version in his submarine series, this time out of a 1952 Cadillac limo.

"It is very long."

1954 "STEEL" CORVETTE

Esterio is a car enthusiast, and he owns more cars than just the Cadillacs he turns into submarines and airplanes. His daily driver is a black 1954 Corvette. According to Corvette expert Noland Adams, it is thought that fewer than ten 1954 models were painted black, but this isn't one of them. Remember, this is Cuba!

And the car appears to have an interesting history.

"This is supposedly the only 1954 Corvette in Cuba," said Esterio, who speaks perfect English. "This car is said to have run in rallies in Italy when it was new. Supposedly it got crashed in one of those rallies, so it was brought back to Cuba. I heard about the car and had hoped to find it."

Years ago, Esterio began asking questions about where a crashed Corvette might be hiding.

Internationally renowned artist and sculptor Segura is also a serious car enthusiast at heart. He has customized Cadillacs and Nashes into submarine and airplane sculptures, but this 'Vette will remain just the way it is.

OPPOSITE TOP: Segura's Corvette's interior is obviously modified, with non-original gauges and steering wheel, diamond-tufted console cover, and drag racing type shifter.

ABOVE: Looking at it through squinted eyes, Esterio Segura's 1954 Corvette could pass for original. But understand that the entire front end, including the hood, was fabricated in metal instead of fiberglass.

RIGHT: The engine in Segura's 'Vette has the correct design, but is not original. He has the original engine in his garage, complete with triple side-draft carbs, which will be reinstalled.

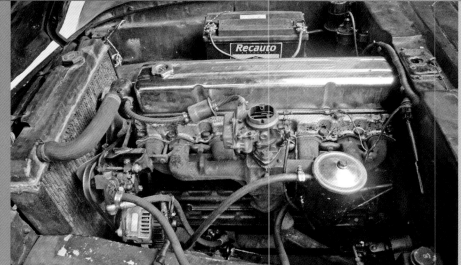

The steel hood appears to have been fabricated from that of a 1957 Ford or Mercury, hammered into a shape that, if you squint, appears to resemble an original Corvette hood and front fenders. The grille, bumpers, and trim were fabricated from scratch, probably from photographs of Corvettes. The windshield is from a later (1956–1962) Corvette.

As with many Cuban cars, if you stand back and look at Esterio's Corvette from a distance, there is something just not quite correct about the car's proportions. The grille, hood, fenders—all seem *similar* to a Corvette, just not on the money. Surely if it were parked next to an original '54 Corvette, the differences would be substantial. But, thankfully for Esterio, this is the only known '54 on the island.

However, while he was living in Spain for a period, a Swiss collector, who lives in Cuba, discovered and purchased the Corvette.

"The car sat in a garage from 1954, when it was crashed, until my friend bought it in 2003," he said. "My friend fixed it, but he is very tall, so he didn't fit in it very well. The Corvette was built for a medium-size guy like me. So I traded him a piece of bronze sculpture for the car in 2010."

It's not clear when the Corvette was repaired, but the damage must have been severe, because all of the bodywork from the firewall forward is fabricated from steel! It goes to illustrate the ingenuity of the Cuban spirit; metal is more plentiful than fiberglass cloth and resin here, so even though steel is much more difficult to fabricate, it was simply the material they had in hand.

Under the hood is a six-cylinder Chevy engine of a similar vintage, but with a single-barrel downdraft carburetor instead of the multi-carb, side-draft setup. Esterio gave us an update on the engine.

"I have a correct Blue Flame six-cylinder engine with three carburetors that is being rebuilt for installation," he said. "Plus the instruments in my car are not original, so I have friends in the US, Miami and New Jersey, who are helping me locate the original pieces."

The car is not Concours d'Elegance caliber, by any means, but it is presentable. And it is, without a doubt, the best 1954 Corvette in Cuba.

QUARTER-MILE CORVETTE

Professionally, René Perez Dominguez promotes concerts and owns a restaurant and a bar, but his passion is for vintage American cars. His favorite is the 1959 Corvette he stores in the small garage behind his beautiful waterfront apartment along the picturesque Malecón.

"I'm not completely sure how this Corvette came to Cuba," said René. "But I bought it about thirteen years ago. I am told that there are four Corvettes in Cuba, and I believe this is the only 1959." He said that he heard about a 1953 Corvette in Santiago, on the other end of the island.

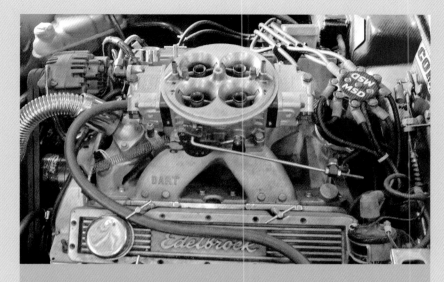

ABOVE: In a country where most cars are powered by diesel tractor engines, René's Corvette engine looks more like one that might frequent a drag strip in the States.

BELOW: René Perez Dominguez shows off his 1959 Corvette. The car has been modified for drag racing, but he retains most of the original equipment.

René's daily driver is this pink 1966 Mercury Comet convertible. He has no idea how the car was allowed to enter Cuba, having been built seven years after the revolution.

René also believes his car was once owned by an auto racing icon. "It is possible that Juan Manuel Fangio may have owned this car," he said. "He imported five 1959 Corvettes into Cuba in 1958. It was the same year he was kidnapped before the start of the Cuban Grand Prix. I was told that some French people living in Cuba at that time bought their Corvettes from him."

René's car is not restored to its original condition, but instead has been "restomodded" for drag racing.

"This car is a performer," he said. "It originally came with a 283-cubic-inch engine, and then had a 327 installed. Now it has been upgraded to a bored and stroked 350-cubic-inch Chevy. The transmission is a Turbo 400, and it has Positraction. It has a Dart intake manifold with a Holley 850 cfm double-pumper."

René told us he had the racing engine built in the United States. (With the US embargo in place for more than fifty years, we wondered how that was possible, but René didn't elaborate.) Clearly he has more disposable income than average Cubans, who struggle to keep their cars operating by using homemade and used parts.

The good news for a future owner is that René still has the original 283 engine, Powerglide transmission, and carburetor that came on the car when new, should someone ever decide to restore the Corvette.

"The engine is there on the stand, and the carb is on the shelf next to the original three-spoke steering wheel."

René's son likes to take the car to the races.

"It looks original, but we bolt on drag slicks once we get to the drag strip," René said. "He races it once or twice a year."

We were told that clandestine speed contests are occasionally held on public roads on the outskirts of Havana.

"On one occasion, I drag raced it, but it was too scary."

René's daily driver is a pink 1965 Mercury Comet convertible with a Russian motor, which he's owned for three years. We asked how an American car built six years after the revolution was allowed to enter the country—he speculated that perhaps somebody in the shipping industry purchased the Comet.

"He probably bought it when his ship was docked in some country that traded with Cuba," René said.

1957 AUSTIN-HEALEY

One of the nicest restored cars we saw on our entire trip was the 100-4 BN4 owned by Dr. Armando S. Miari de Casas, the president of the Club de Autos Deportivos de Cuba—the largest sports car club in the country. Armando is a mechanical engineer and university professor, so he took the restoration of his Healey to an academic level.

"I restored the car myself, working with a small team of enthusiasts," he said. "I've owned it for about five years."

Armando told us it was a complete car when he got it, but in very poor condition.

"I bought it from the old man who was the original owner," he said. "He was a doctor and bought the car new in 1958. When it broke down in 1993, it sat in his garage until I bought it in 2010."

Armando said the hardest part about restoring the car was welding patches on the bottom of the doors, which he did himself: "The old man installed [nonoriginal] backup lights, which I left on because they are part of the car's history."

The exhaust system was also a big fabrication challenge because of the car's low ground clearance.

"Now it is the best Austin-Healey in Cuba," he said proudly. "It is original down to the last screw. That is certainly a rarity in a country where cars are patched

Engineer and educator Armando owns this Austin-Healey 100-4 BN4, one of the nicest restored cars we saw on our trip.

Armando entered his Healey in an annual sports-car road rally.

together with parts from other cars, and even household items, in order to keep them operating.

"I rebuilt the engine as well. In Cuba, if you want to restore a car, you must work with every original nut, bolt, and part, because there are no replacements."

Armando's job as a professor allows him some freedom to travel outside of the country, including visits to relatives in Austin, Texas, and Miami, Florida. So he has visited stores such as Home Depot, Harbor Freight, and Advance Auto. He knows exactly what he is missing.

Five years ago, Armando knew nothing about Austin-Healeys. "Now every mechanic in Cuba who is working on an Austin-Healey or an MG or a Triumph calls me with their problems," he said. He mentioned that there are fourteen Austin-Healeys in Cuba including his, most of them Bugeye Sprites.

"And there is one Mini Cooper in Cuba," he said.

Armando mentioned that his brother is restoring a Healey Silverstone, which is a rare car regardless of what country in which it resides. Unfortunately, we were not able to arrange a visit to that car during our stay.

Armando's Healey is his first sports car. Before this car, he owned a 1952 Chevrolet that he inherited from his father. At one time he also owned a VW Beetle and a Harley-Davidson motorcycle.

Now that his Healey is restored and operating well, he has another project in line: he found and bought a second Austin-Healey that he would like to modify. Obviously he has a little hot-rodder in his blood.

"I would like to install a V-motor," he said. "I don't care if it's a V-6 or a V-8."

1958 PORSCHE
356 CARRERA

One of the most interesting car guys we met in Cuba was Ivan Celestrin, a lawyer and Cuba's resident Porsche guru. Ivan was born in Cuba but was sent by his parents to live in Moscow when he was a little boy.

"I didn't know a word of Russian when I moved there," he said about attending school there as a child. "Now I'm fluent."

He eventually moved back to Cuba and went to college, then law school, and became a lawyer.

"The first time I saw a Porsche 356 in my life was in the American movie *Top Gun*, with Tom Cruise," said Ivan. "In the movie, Tom's girlfriend, Kelly McGinnis, drove a Porsche Speedster.

"Then in another movie, *48 Hours*, there was another 356."

The hook was set, and it began a lifelong passion in Ivan for the brand from Stuttgart, Germany. As luck would have it, when Ivan was married, his new father-in-law owned two Porsches: a Speedster and a Super 90 coupe.

"The Porsche I own once sat in the showroom in Havana until after the revolution," he said of his own car, a 1956 356 Carrera GS. "The Porsche sat

Ivan Celestrin's Porsche four-cam Carrera is being restored in this "shop." What you can't see is the stink of the pigpen to the left.

for forty-five years and only had about twenty-five thousand to thirty thousand kilometers until I bought it. Under its first owner, the car raced along the Malecón as car number sixteen."

Porsche Carreras are very rare. The car was named to celebrate the brand's victories in Mexico's Carrera Panamericana road races in 1953 and 1954. As opposed to standard Porsche 356s with pushrod engines, the Carreras are powered by the same four-cam motor that had been developed for the 550 Spyder. Only 1,138 were built between 1955 and 1963.

Ivan and his wife actually owned two Carreras during their marriage, which would be an impressive collection if they lived in Beverly Hills, but much more so in Havana, Cuba. When he and his wife divorced, she got one of them. But Ivan got custody of their wonderful daughter, Cecelia, which to us seemed like a terrific trade.

Ivan offered to take us to see his car, which was undergoing restoration at a nearby shop. In the States, restoration shops are usually clean, well-organized buildings stocked with machinery and a staff of uniform-wearing professionals. In Cuba, they are quite different. Actually, calling them "shops" is really pushing it.

The open-air restoration facility handling Ivan's rare Porsche was at the end of a very rocky road on the outskirts of Havana, where a top speed of 10 miles per hour was pushing it. We arrived at a house that, for Cuban standards, was very nice. We beeped the horn and someone came to open the gate; driving down the driveway, we saw several restoration projects that were parked and awaiting attention. At the front of the line was Ivan's 356.

There was no "shop" to speak of—just a flat, corrugated roof over a concrete floor. Walls are

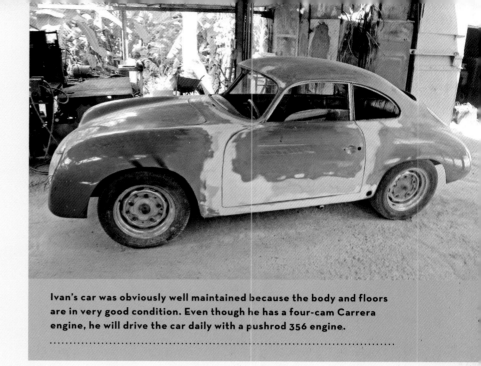

Ivan's car was obviously well maintained because the body and floors are in very good condition. Even though he has a four-cam Carrera engine, he will drive the car daily with a pushrod 356 engine.

not too important here because of the heat, but it was what was next to the driveway that didn't fit: a pigpen.

No, really—a pigpen with all the stench that accompanies pigs when they are lying in the mud. This was ten feet from where Ivan's valuable Porsche was being prepared for paint.

Anyway, the Porsche was a steely metallic blue when new, but Ivan was having it painted black.

It needed some rust repair in the battery area under the hood and a small area behind the seat, but otherwise the car was in sound condition.

We decided that we would love to see how this car comes out when it is painted black, because, as you probably know, black cars need perfect bodywork to look correct.

Ivan was rightfully proud of his car. He told us the price he was paying for bodywork and paint: CUC$500, or about US$500. That is the total cost for labor and materials! "I hope the bodywork and paint is finished in the next seven days," Ivan said.

Next we followed him to an upholstery shop a few miles away.

ABOVE: The upholstery shop that was reupholstering Ivan's Porsche interior is also stitching new hides for his 1947 Chevy convertible.

BELOW RIGHT: This is not Ivan's car, but another Cuban Porsche 356 A, which is awaiting restoration.

to an alternator, and a power brake booster had been added.

Cervando showed us Ivan's completed Porsche seats, which looked very nice. They were done in a high-quality, dark brown vinyl in the original pattern. The black car with brown interior should look very handsome.

"There is a small group of Porsche owners in Cuba," said Ivan. "Originally there were thirty-nine or forty Porsches in the country before the revolution, but there are only about eight or nine remaining.

"I know of another 356 in Cuba, a 1500 Super, and it has roller bearings, but it's not a four-cam. Then there is another guy who has two 356s, and a Brazilian who has lived in Cuba for twenty years, who also has a 356."

Ivan is satisfied with his Porsche, a car that is rare and desirable in any country. And even though the car may not be restored to Porsche Club of America standards, this one will certainly be the best Porsche Carrera in Cuba.

"I like to do the mechanical work," said Ivan, "but I prefer specialists to handle each area."

We arrived at the upholstery shop, which was owned by Ivan's friend Cervando. Sitting in front of the shop was a *bright* green 1948 Chevy convertible that was receiving a full custom interior and a new convertible top—and, actually, the quality of the workmanship and materials was about as good as any hot-rod shop in the States could produce. The Chevy's upholstery was being done in white vinyl with lime-green piping to match the car's exterior. It had a standard six-cylinder engine under the hood, but it had been converted from a generator

1958 MERCEDES-BENZ 190SL

Ivan Celestrin's daily driver is a spiffy silver '58 Mercedes 190SL. It looks correct from the outside but has a two-liter engine with a two-barrel downdraft carburetor under the hood. The engine is not correct.

"On Monday I found an original 190 engine here in Cuba," Ivan said. "It has the correct dual carburetors, so I'll rebuild that and put it in my car. Anything is possible with engines here in Cuba."

Ivan is a car guy's car guy. Over the past few years, and during our most recent trip, he spent days introducing us to other car enthusiasts and shops that specialize in the care and restoration of old cars. He also invited us to his house to inspect his spare Porsche parts inventory and treated us to a wonderful dinner at an outdoor cafe along the Malecón.

He and his daughter, Cecelia, were perfect automotive diplomats for our threesome of old-car enthusiasts from the United States. We certainly hope to one day return the favor in our country, Ivan.

Ivan's daily driver is this Mercedes-Benz 190 SL. The car is powered by a non-original Mercedes four-cylinder engine, but the day before we arrived, he found a correct 190 SL, complete with side-draft carbs.

THE RED CONNECTION

During the Cold War, Russia had a huge presence in Cuba. This relationship lasted until the Soviet Union collapsed and the cost of propping up the Cuban economy became more than what the Russians needed or wanted. Although Russian Ladas are very common in Havana as a result of that relationship, no self-respecting commissar would be seen being squired around in one. The car of choice for the high-ranking "Ruskies" was the GAZ Chaika, a Chrysler-esque limo with a 4.7-liter V-8 and a very fifties crushed-velour and leather interior.

During our first trip to Cuba in 2009, on the road that passes in front of the Plaza de la Revolución there was—and the operative word is "was"—a huge shed with fifteen of the Chaikas that remained when the Russians bailed out. With fuel at a premium, the cars were getting engine swaps: four-cylinder diesels were filling the cavernous voids once occupied by the big V-8s.

As we were driving by, we asked our tour guide, Abel, to swing around so that we could get a good look and shoot some photos of the proletariat's limos. The shedded area was fenced in, so we asked Abel if we could shoot some photos up close. He told us it was impossible. However, even in a Communist country (perhaps especially in a Communist country), a few dollars can very often gain access. We requested that Abel negotiate for us, and upon returning to our van, he advised that for CUC$10 (about US$10) we could photograph to our heart's content—which we did. We were surprised to see one of the mechanics wearing a Jacksonville Jaguars T-shirt and pleased to see an MGA on blocks awaiting a restoration.

Upon examining the Chaikas and shooting all the photos we needed, we asked Abel who we should pay. He directed us to get in the van and pass the cash to him between the two front seats, which we did. He then shook the hand of our host and palmed the lucre to him. While driving away, we asked what that was all about. His answer was simple: "We were being watched." By who we do not know, but welcome to Cuba.

OPPOSITE PAGE, ABOVE, AND BELOW: Rows of Russian Chaikas remain in Cuba decades after the Soviets left the island. It was against the law for us to take a photo of these cars, except if we paid $10—then we were allowed.

300SLS, DOUBLE BUBBLES, AND OTHER RARITIES

Our contact Quico purchased a 300SL in 1962. He still owns it today!

"It belonged to a person who left the country after the Revolution," he said. "It belonged to Batista's minister of public works. The car was confiscated and the government sold it to me when I was a young man.

"My car was driven by Abelardo Carreras in one of the Grand Prix races. These days, our lives don't allow us to be as close to the cars as we would like."

Alongside the Gullwing were a 300SL Roadster in similar shape, a 1956 Ford Crown Victoria under restoration, a Fiat Abarth 750 "Double Bubble," the remains of an American sprint car, a Healey Silverstone, and our personal favorite: a very rare Chrysler Ghia Special Coupe, one of twelve made in 1953.

Quico said that there are another 300SL coupe and another 300SL roadster still on the island. The second coupe is rumored to be owned by one of Castro's right-hand men—unfortunately, he got on the wrong side of Fidel, which, apparently is not all that hard to do, and was put in jail for a number of years. Now in his eighties, he has lost his sight, and his daughter inherited the coupe and an Uhlenhaut

Once a gleaming, new sports car, this Gullwing was entered in one of the early Cuban Grands Prix.

ABOVE: Cleaned of the debris that had covered it for decades, this 300SL roadster appears to be in restorable condition, but in Cuba, access to rare bits and pieces, such as correct taillights, will be nearly impossible.

BELOW RIGHT: Have you ever seen a sadder sight?

sedan, which are both in hiding. We've seen these cars in photos, but not in person.

Quico, who is one of the most "wired" car guys in Cuba, also told us about several other cars that were once seen regularly.

"There were once three BMW 507s in Cuba," he said. "One was white, one red, and one black. There is still one remaining. And there is an Aston Martin on the island. They installed a Russian Volga motor in it—to me, they destroyed it. The last time I saw it, it was in very poor condition.

"And I believe there is a Jaguar XKSS here, but I'm not sure where. Recently it was confirmed that a third XKSS was shipped to Cuba."

Previously, only two XKSSs were believed to have been shipped to Cuba, and those two were exported by the British collector Colin Crabbe more than forty years ago. If a XKSS still exists on the island, that means three must have been originally imported. But Jaguar expert Terry Larson advises that all sixteen XKSSs are

accounted for—though he does not discount any rumors, chances are there were only two in Cuba, and they are no longer there.

"There is also a Ferrari Testa Rossa 'Red Head' body without a chassis sitting in Havana," said Quico. "And I've heard there is a Ferrari here with a Chevy engine in it."

We also met a man named Jolvany, who said he had seen interesting cars hidden away.

"I have seen exclusive cars that are hiding," he told us. "I have seen a never-touched 1959 Chrysler and also a 1959 Buick that was purchased new and never driven."

This Chrysler Ghia was built in 1953 and probably shipped to Cuba for one of the car shows that took place in the country in the 1950s.

CHRYSLER GHIA

Quico said that there are many stories that have circulated about this car.

"One story was that it was owned by the owner of the Lincoln-Mercury dealership in Havana," he said. "A man named McNoul owns the car now."

The Chrysler Special Ghia is as handsome as they get. Twelve were built and eleven are accounted for in the United States and Europe. In all probability, this is the "twelfth man" on the field.

(By the way, the Cubans now access the Internet and know the value of their cars. We were shown printouts of the sale of similar cars.)

ABOVE: When new, this Chrysler Ghia, with a Chrysler New Yorker chassis, was wrapped with an absolutely stunning body by Carrozzeria Ghia in Italy.

BELOW: The Ghia's once-supple leather-upholstered interior is now a storage shed for engine parts. Sad.

RIGHTFUL OWNERS

The white BMW 507 belonged (or perhaps still belongs) to the father of our friend Dick Morales, now living in Jacksonville, Florida. The Morales family owned a successful construction contracting business in Havana, and Dick and his wife took the 507 on their honeymoon (pictured).

In 1960, after "the triumph of the revolution," the Morales family fled to Florida, eventually settling in Jacksonville.

Now here is the rub. The Morales family still owned the car when they fled Cuba. According to Cuban law, if you have not claimed ownership in twenty years, the car is no longer yours. As with the property abandoned in Germany during World War II, could the BMW 507 still be claimed by the family, should business relationships be resumed between Cuba and the United States?

On a larger scale, Bacardi could very well claim the facilities the revolution confiscated. Suppose someone bought the 507 in good faith and brought it to the United States—could the family claim ownership then?

These are all questions that international legal authorities will have to address. Recent court rulings involving a Mercedes-Benz 540K and a Ferrari 375 MM are still under review or appeal. In short, you could very well purchase a car in Cuba from an individual who does not have the legal right to sell it. If the rumors that the car still exists in Cuba are true, who is the rightful owner?

—Bill Warner

RIGHT AND BELOW: Dick Morales and his new wife, Marcia, prepare to leave their wedding reception in Havana in their rare BMW 507 sports car. When they escaped Cuba for the United States in 1960, they left their beloved BMW behind. The question is: If relations between the United States and Cuba are normalized, and the car still exists, would the Morales family have claim to it?

PORSCHE 550 SPYDER

As our plane approached the Havana airport on our first trip to Cuba in 2009, we noticed a "road course" off to the left side of the airplane. It appeared to be a small Sebring- or Lime Rock–type of racetrack, but then it flashed out of view as the plane turned for the landing.

We made it our mission to find out more about that racing circuit.

It turns out it was a go-kart track. We will discuss the track itself in more detail elsewhere in this book, but it was there that we met an interesting gentleman, Chris Baker—a Brit living in Cuba. Baker married a Cuban woman and decided to relocate

from England's frosty and wet weather to Cuba's more temperate climate. He had a small trailer behind his Mercedes-Benz station wagon that he used to tow his racing kart to the track. Baker told us a fascinating story about spotting a rare Porsche in Havana traffic one day.

"I can tell you exactly," he said. "It was very close to the Tropicana nightclub about seven or eight years ago [2000 or 2001]. I was stopped at a traffic light on a Saturday morning and turned my head and said, 'Whoa.' It was a Porsche 550 Spyder. I couldn't, or wouldn't, turn around—I don't remember. There must have been a woman involved.

"Anyway, I remember the body was in raw aluminum. I never saw or heard of it again."

Great story. We had hoped to learn more about the car during our 2015 trip and asked Quico, who

We never actually laid our eyes on these cars, but shot a photo of a photo of the two hidden cars—a rare Cisitalia (foreground) and a 1954 Buick Skylark. In 1954, Skylarks were only available as convertibles, so this is either a rare prototype or a "Cuban special."

During our 2015 trip to Cuba, we met Mark Monson, a Canadian from Toronto who has lived in Havana for forty years. He owns this pretty MGA and just bought a 1956 Chevy.

is very connected in the racing world, to shed a little more light on the Spyder.

"There is only one Spyder in Cuba, but possibly two engines," he said. "The man does not want to sell it. He works around the world for the embassy and doesn't want anyone to know what he has. In two years, he will retire and begin to enjoy the car. The same man also owns a Healey Silverstone [possibly the one in the shed alongside the Chrysler Special], which is missing the original engine."

Quico told us the car was originally owned by the president of Shell Oil Company and that it was never raced.

LICENSE PLATES

We found out that the colors of license plates tell a lot about the ownership of a vehicle.

If a plate has blue markings on the left side, the vehicle is owned by the government; if those markings are black, the vehicle is privately owned. If they are green, it is owned by the army.

There is something just so special about a vintage Jaguar Mark 9 sedan, with a partial Mercedes grill, that doubles as a taxi cab.

"A friend of the original owner wanted to race it, but the owner wouldn't allow it. It is in very good condition and has the long headrest."

Baker said that he had heard of an Italian guy living on the island who owned a Maserati. "I heard he died, but the car is supposedly still around. I have never seen it, though."

He said he has also heard about other Ferraris and Maseratis but has never seen them either.

HISPANO-SUIZA

Little is known about a Hispano-Suiza that showed up in one of the British journals. When first reported, it was a body sitting in the middle of a sugar plantation. The next time we saw a photo of it, it was exposed in an X-ray of a shipping container showing the car complete with engine and chassis but in really poor shape. We were told the authorities seized the car, and where it is now is anybody's guess.

CLASSICS FOR LADAS

"I have a pain in my heart about all the valuable cars that were taken out of Cuba," said Quico. He was referring to a company called Coaches Classico. In 1980, the cash-strapped Cuban government partnered with the UK-based agency, which allowed Cuban citizens to trade their old, often impractical cars for brand new Russian Ladas.

The program came to an end when people started to complain that their cars were worth a lot more than the Ladas they were receiving in return. That's when the cars became designated national treasures and were no longer permitted to leave the country.

It is estimated that hundreds of Cuba's most valuable cars left the country during that period and now sit in the hands of wealthy collectors around the world.

ONES THAT GOT AWAY

Rumors of rare and valuable cars hidden across Cuba are rampant. It seems that many enthusiasts who have visited the country have stories about owners of classic cars who are waiting until the political climate is right before bringing their treasures out of the shadows.

One story that has kept renowned collector Richie Clyne awake at night is the rumor of a garage full of Rolls-Royce Silver Ghosts.

"I saw a photo with a bunch of Ghosts," he said. "[Brit car hunter] John Warth showed me photos of seventeen of them on a farm. I heard they would cost US$1.6 million to buy at the time, but it would take another $100,000 to get them out of the country on boats.

"But John flew back to England for a few weeks and never returned to Cuba, so that's all I know. He died and I never found out anything else about the Ghosts. All I remember is that they were photographed in a Quonset hut."

So Clyne went to the expense of renting a plane and a pilot to fly him around the country, looking for a Quonset hut large enough to store seventeen Rolls-Royces.

"We'd fly across Cuba every few weeks. My eyes would be pressed against the windshield, looking for Quonset huts below," he said. But he never found them.

"Cuba is definitely the last frontier of the old car world," said Clyne.

TWO CORVETTES THAT GOT AWAY

Quico's friend Albert was a real car guy, and he spoke perfect English, which was rare. We met him at a sports car rally, and he told us he attended the Sebring Formula One race in 1959.

Albert told us a story about a 1958 Corvette he purchased new in Miami and had shipped to Cuba on the ferryboat SS *Florida*.

"It was white with red interior and had a fuel-injected 283 engine with a Duntov cam," said Albert. "It made 290 horsepower. I bought it with a four-speed, [a] heavy-duty suspension, and a [Positraction] rear. I raced it some.

"I kept it until 1961, when I was getting married. It had 30,000 miles on it."

Later Albert bought another 'Vette.

"When I worked at the airport, I bought another '58, also fuel injected. It was blue and gray, had a four-speed, and had a blue interior. I saw it at the airport and bought it in 1974 from the original owner. I sold it in 1982 when fuel became too expensive. Both my Corvettes are no longer on the island."

Albert didn't elaborate on how the cars were sold and shipped from Cuba.

—Tom Cotter

8

RUNNING ON ★ EMPTY: REPAIR SHOPS IN THE STREETS

PRIOR TO 2010, EDUARDO MESEJO MAESTRE, DIRECTOR OF THE DEPÓSITO DEL AUTOMÓVIL—HAVANA'S ANTIQUE CAR MUSEUM—HAD NEVER BEEN TO A PROPER AUTO-PARTS STORE AS WE KNOW THEM IN THE STATES. THE AUTO-PARTS "CHAIN" IN CUBA IS CALLED SASA, AND IT PROVIDES BASIC AUTO PARTS TO RESIDENTS. THE CHAIN IS OPERATED BY THE COMMITTEES FOR THE DEFENSE OF THE REVOLUTION, AN ARM OF THE CUBAN GOVERNMENT. THERE ARE TWELVE SASA STORES ACROSS THE COUNTRY.

You fix it where it breaks! When a car breaks down, Cuban drivers can't call AAA for a tow truck. The driver of this Chevy is trying to get it fired up again. *Walter Bibikow/Getty Images*

The stores are small and neat, but not very well stocked. Until he visited the United States, this is what Eduardo believed was an average auto-parts store. Then he was invited to Jacksonville, Florida, on a cultural exchange to participate as a judge at the 2010 Amelia Island Concours d'Elegance. During that trip, he visited an Advance Auto Parts store and walked around with his mouth agape. Instead of there being just a few quarts of oil on the shelves, there were dozens of types, and varieties of viscosities, both synthetic and organic!

Rows of shelves neatly stacked with batteries, car waxes, light bulbs, tools, and on and on. And there were dozens of pints of brake fluid, a chemical in short supply in Cuba.

He was in shock.

We Americans are spoiled. Within a mile of any suburban center, we'll usually have an Auto Zone, an Advance Auto, and a NAPA store. Cubans, on the other hand, must search far and wide to find the right part—or one that will work in its place. Parts are so scarce in Cuba that when

The owner of this Plymouth taxi makes repairs to his front end in a traffic lane. And no jack stands in sight!

word gets out that a car has been in an accident or was taken off the road, mechanics rush to the scene in an attempt to buy or barter for the parts. Chemicals such as oil are recycled after major engine repairs because replacement fluids are expensive and in short supply. Our translator, Abe, told us that the SASA store is where you can buy both new and used parts, and even new cars, if anybody could actually afford one.

"Occasionally there are as many as a dozen engines lined up on the floor for sale," said Abe. But when we walked into one of the SASA stores in Havana, there was only one engine for sale, a Renault unit that had previously powered a front-wheel-drive car. Nobody could tell us what model it had been removed from, but our bet is on a later-model car because it was extremely clean. We were told it probably had been shipped from France.

The asking price was CUC$2,436.15—not terrible. We learned that brand-new engines were also for sale for between CUC$6,000 and $7,000.

Imagine trying to convert this front-wheel-drive engine to power, say, a rear-wheel-drive 1953 Cadillac convertible. What gearbox would you use? How would you make the bellhousing adaptor? Would an early clutch assembly work with a modern flywheel? These challenges had us scratching our heads, and thinking about them further convinced us that Cuban mechanics are amazing self-taught engineers.

Looking at the SASA showcases allowed us to see some of the accessories they sold: steering wheels and steering wheel covers; spray paint; speakers; light bulbs; stereos; lug wrenches; antennas; mirrors; Ferrari decals (a popular item, and about every third car we saw had them displayed, regardless of brand); and a number of VW Beetle parts, which explained the huge number of non-Volkswagens driving around with Beetle taillights mounted.

ROLLING ACCESSORY DISPLAYS

In an effort to individualize their cars, Cuban owners of vintage American cars sure like accessories—the gaudier the better. And because the selection is so limited in their country, we saw many of the same items over and over again.

Most popular are the previously mentioned Ferrari decals, which because of their low cost might appear in several locations and in several different sizes on the same car. Another popular add-on is the late-1950s Chrysler Imperial "sparrow strainer" taillight, which has a Flash Gordon–esque rocket ship design surrounded by a vertical "halo." The nickname comes from the fact that a small bird, such as a sparrow, could be squished between the components.

ABOVE: Speaking of George Barris, this Mercury trolling the streets of Havana looks like a white canvas for the Kustom King to ply his talents on top-chopping and lowering.

BELOW: You can imagine how the taillight got its name, but it makes one wonder how many sparrows actually lost their lives as a result of coming in contact in the 1950s.

Multiple antennas are also a popular treatment, although we're not sure customizer George Barris would think very highly of that modification. When the hood of a vintage American car in Cuba is open, you can see other popular chrome accessories: valve covers and air cleaners. Of course, multiple Buick-style "portholes" are always in fashion, whether mounted on an actual Buick, on a Henry J, or on a Corvair.

Other popular bolt-on items include American Racing–style five-spoke mag wheels that resemble the original Torq Thrust design. These wheels make almost any car in America look better, and they do the same thing to Cuban cars. We spoke to the owner of a 1953 Mercury who had just installed a new set of chrome American Racing wheels and wide whitewalls. He told us he traveled to Mexico City and bought them for $1,000.

Similarly, it's not unusual to see a 1951 Chevy with what look like Mercedes-Benz factory wheels. Like in the States, aftermarket wheels are important to Cubans.

ABOVE: Another Lada, this stretch limousine shows again how innovative Cuban mechanics can be. Most likely, this was produced from two Ladas, one crashed in the front, another from the rear. It's a whole lotta Lada.

BELOW: Equipped with all the accessories that can fit, this Russian Lada must be the envy of many young Cuban car enthusiasts.

THESE CARS ARE SMOKERS

Look at the average vintage American car cruising the Cuban streets, and the chances are that it's smoking. And not just little puffs, but huge plumes of dark smoke that can momentarily make the back of the car disappear until it dissipates.

Breathing in this city can be hazardous to your health.

Seen from the roof of our hotel, the Parque Central in Havana, the gray-brown smog resembled those awful photos we've all seen of downtown Los Angeles before smog requirements were mandated on cars and factories. There are no emission laws in Cuba that penalize motorists, or factories for that matter, for pumping tons of pollution particulates into the air, and it made us wonder how many days we were shortening our lives by taking breaths of the dirty air.

Aside from the human health concerns, the cars themselves are unhealthy as well. The reason for these unburned hydrocarbons and diesel fumes pluming out of a car's tailpipe is one of two things: either the piston rings and cylinders are totally worn out, or the car has been converted to aging diesel power.

Finding new piston rings for a sixty-year-old car is hard enough if you live in Pennsylvania or Oregon, but finding new rings in Cuba is next to impossible. So what to do? A Cuban owner could attempt to have a set of rings shipped from the United States through a third country, such as Mexico. When the new parts arrive, the challenge is then gaining access to a competent machinist with boring and honing equipment.

So, because of the expense and trouble of rebuilding a vintage engine—never mind the down time during the rebuild—this route is often a troublesome option. As a result, many owners leave the original engine in place, despite the smoke.

Unless . . .

DID GM PUT DIESELS IN '55 CHEVYS?

We spent several days with our friend Quico, a terrific man who heads whatever motorsport activity takes place in Cuba. We met with Quico and his friend Albert at a road rally, the largest motorsport activity currently held on the island. Albert was an amazing resource on cars and racing in Cuba and could answer our questions in English.

We asked him why so many vintage cars here have straight front axles and what appear to be industrial rear ends. It's common to notice familiar old models sitting at an unfamiliar ride height compared to stock. And the front and rear suspensions seem to be too narrow, especially when mounted under a huge car such as a Cadillac or an Oldsmobile.

Another mechanic had told us that the suspension components were actually sourced

Russian, or Belarusian, diesel engines—usually sourced from elderly tractors—are used to power everything from front-engined Corvairs to this Chrysler.

Vintage car enthusiasts who walk across the street to look under the hood of an old American car are nearly always disappointed to find a diesel Russian engine residing in the engine bay.

from Russian Volga automobiles. "You can buy the Volga engines directly from the government," the mechanic, Pastor, had said. This made some sense, because finding replacement parts—bearings, seals, brakes, ball joints, and so on—for a later-model Volga would certainly be easier than sourcing those same parts for a dozen different sixty-year-old makes and models, especially with the close ties that Cuba and Russia had for nearly half a century.

But something didn't add up. When we inspected the many Volgas we saw on the streets, we found that none of them had straight front axles or the industrial rear ends like the ones we had seen on so many cars on the road. That's why it was so helpful to talk to Albert.

"They are from tractors and trucks," he said. "Belarus shipped seventy thousand diesel tractors to Cuba. Those have been dismantled, and the suspension components and engines are used to keep our cars on the road." Finally, an answer that made sense.

And an explanation for why so many of the cars rattled and smoked so profusely.

TAILLIGHT DIPLOMACY

The US trade embargo doesn't allow American companies to sell much-needed parts to the Cuban motorists who desperately need them. Richard Shnitzler has found a way around that issue. Shnitzler's organization, called TailLight Diplomacy, formed under the aegis of the United States–Cuba Sister City Association, encourages American car enthusiasts to send Cubans their "used" parts, which circumvents the embargo laws. Parts the organization helps send include sparkplugs, carburetors, brake components, repair manuals, and engine pieces such as pistons, which are often discarded by American restorers.

Shnitzler said that the parts are invaluable and will help keep Cuban cars on the road for another half century.

And just how did a pink 1962 Pontiac convertible find its way to Cuba during the embargo? This Poncho engine long ago bit the dust, and a Russian diesel engine now powers this car.

Resembling a Gasser drag racer, this overcrowded wagon has a tractor front suspension with two parallel leaf springs installed.

BLOOD FROM A STONE

Cubans are generally poor, whether they participate in the underground economy or not. So, because they don't have a lot of excess cash, and because proper car parts and supplies are not readily available, they have to make do.

During our 2009 trip, we figured that Cubans must subscribe to an extreme recycling philosophy and that, as a result, junkyards must do a brisk business. Plus, who knows what cool old stuff might be hiding in a proper junkyard? Our minds went to aluminum-bodied Jaguars and Maserati Grand Prix cars.

But our tour guide, Abel, had no idea what we were talking about.

"What's a junkyard?" he asked.

"You know, it's where old cars go after they are no longer usable. And you can buy the old parts."

Abel looked confused, then said, "My friends, my whole country is a junkyard."

Now we were the confused ones. But eventually we realized what Abel was trying to tell us: there is no such thing as a junkyard in Cuba because nothing ever totally wears out! Parts are used virtually forever, then are stored by the owner when finally worn out, potentially to be used as trading fodder with another mechanic.

Abel laughed as he told us about all the years he has been a tour guide in Cuba. He is often asked by foreign tourists to take them to churches, historical sites, beaches, museums, cigar or rum factories, even to brothels. "My friends, you are my first clients to ask me to take them to a junkyard!"

POLISH FIATS

Some of the most popular non-American cars cruising the Cuban streets are the Polski Fiats. These are Fiats built under license in Poland and used in many former Soviet bloc countries. They are powered by rear-mounted, two-cylinder, air-cooled engines, and you can identify them by their high-pitched exhaust sound even before seeing them.

These cars are popular among young Cubans, and we regularly saw them sporting spoilers, mag wheels, and wild colors. They are to Cuba what the Trabant was to East Germany: cheap, basic transportation.

Obviously Abel hadn't heard of El Relámpago, a General Motors dealership that also owned the largest junkyard and parts house in Cuba in the 1950s. But that was decades before he was born.

Abel told us the two rules of auto repair in his country: "Rule number one, the Cuban way is to do whatever you need to do to keep your car running.

"And rule number two, refer to rule number one."

MAKING A SILK PURSE OUT OF A SOW'S EAR

As we've seen, Cubans must make do. When they can't find exactly the correct part or supply to repair their car, they find something that will work.

"The Cuban people can paint a car under a tree or in the street," said Abel. Which, after driving around Havana for a couple of days, we actually witnessed.

Of course well-heeled Cubans might actually prefer that their cars be painted in a proper spray booth with filtration and downdraft, but that would be the minority.

When we visited the SASA auto-parts store, we noticed a limited selection of spray paint in various colors, so we deduced that was a common method of Cubans painting their classic rides. But we also heard of another popular method: the "Cuban Way," as Abel was fond of saying.

We were told that some Cubans paint their cars by dabbing a sponge in a jar of paint and brushing it on the car's body. This often leaves an uneven and blotchy finish—so how do they buff out the cars afterward?

"Toothpaste is the best car polish," said Eduardo Mesejo, the museum director.

Other "Cuban Way" methods of car repair and maintenance?

"We use Coca-Cola to break rusted bolts and nuts free," Eduardo said.

And to keep old tires looking nice and black?

"We use water and sugar. We put four or five tablespoons of sugar into the water, wipe it on the tire, and wait. Or else you take an old inner tube and soak it in diesel fluid. Then light it on fire and wait until it melts. When you wipe the hot liquid on the tires, they become black as night."

We're lucky in America; we can just go to the auto-parts store and buy a bottle of Armor All.

NECESSITY IS THE MOTHER OF INVENTION

There was an amazing story broadcast on National Public Radio about a Cuban mechanic who either couldn't find or couldn't afford a set of piston rings he needed for his vintage engine. So he found an old piece of cast-iron plumbing pipe the approximate diameter of his piston. Using a hacksaw, he carefully cut slices of the pipe, then used a file to make his own piston rings in the proper diameter.

Amazing.

Brake fluid is something else that's expensive and in short supply in Cuba. Inventive Cubans have a solution for that as well, Eduardo told us.

"We use shampoo in the brake lines. It contains silicone and works good at slow speeds."

(The lesson to be learned here is not to step in front of a moving Cuban car.)

Not sure what the United States Department of Transportation would think about that, but it seems to be working in Cuba.

When the owner of this Chrysler decided he needed more room for his taxi service, he simply cut the roof from another car and applied it to the top of his car. "Taxi!"

TWO KINDS OF CHROME

Ivan, the Porsche owner (see page 112), brought us to a friend's chrome shop in downtown Havana. He explained to us that there are several such shops in Cuba, but this one was the best.

Manuel's chrome and polishing shop does work on some of the higher-end restoration projects going on in the Havana area. In addition to chroming, the owner also does welding, fabrication, and mechanical repair.

His shop was different from the others we had visited. It was very neat, without a lot of junk lying around in the corners. Clearly Manuel was very proud of his work. He had a series of tanks that allowed him to apply various finishes, such as copper, onto the metal surface before the actual chrome is applied.

Manuel's personal project was a very nice 1956 Chevy restomod, which was one of the best cars we saw on the island. Obviously he makes good money and has good connections, because the exceptional white and turquoise Chevy is equipped with a 305-cubic-inch engine, a four-barrel carb mounted on a high-rise manifold, chrome headers, a billet front-drive system, electronic gauges, a GM 700R automatic transmission with verdrive, power disc brakes, and polished American Racing Torq Thrust wheels.

Most cars in Cuba are not prepared to 20 percent of this Chevy's specifications.

Four-door sedans rule in Cuba! This fuchsia-colored 1956 Chevy taxi can't be missed as it cruises the streets seeking customers.

TAXI!

In the United States, two-door coupes are always in higher demand among enthusiasts, but in Cuba, four-doors rule. Four-door sedans, you see, can more easily be used as a taxicab than a two-door, and taxis are what most of these vintage American cars have become. These taxis are usually overflowing with passengers, packed with residents on their way to work, home, or shopping. Residents can commute for just a few pesos a day, far less than the taxi rates for tourists.

Tourist taxis are often pretty, colorful convertibles—though many we saw were in fact chopped two-door sedans or hardtops. (We had to check the windshield headers or look for a folded top to tell for sure.) These cabs usually take visitors for a CUC$35 one-hour sightseeing tour around the city. "Excuse me, would you like a ride?" asked the owner of a bright red 1959 Buick Special convertible, which he used to transport guests around the city. "It has original engine," he added, as if that would steer more tourists in his direction.

Some Cuban taxi owners charge money if tourists take photos next to their cars. They definitely charge if the tourist wants to have their photo taken in the driver's seat.

We were told that private taxi drivers must pay the government CUC$45 a day as the fee for picking up passengers. Once that fee is paid, and the fuel purchased, everything else is profit.

ABOVE: Hailing a cab in Havana can result in any number of vehicles. This horse-drawn cab is a popular option for tourists visiting the city.

BELOW: Maxi-Taxi—Scenes like this are visible every day in the Cuban countryside. Citizens who cannot afford a car are herded like cattle into trucks like this.

COCO CABS

There are also popular little three-wheeled tourist taxis that scoot around town at nearly full speed. These are the tiny Coco Cabs, which are powered by a single-cylinder lawn mower–type engine. They are distinctive because of their round fiberglass bodies, which resemble large yellow coconuts.

GRANCAR

We visited a company called Grancar, which is a taxi and drivetrain conversion company that operates out of an open-air garage. Because of the summer heat and the temperate conditions in the winter, walls are not necessary.

"We install front and rear suspensions out of

Coco Cabs can be seen zipping all over the city. The exhaust makes a tinny sound and usually spews smoke, but they are a certainly an efficient method of getting across town. *ArtMarie/Getty Images*

It is now possible for tourists to rent "restored" American cars to tour around the island. This 1957 Ford is an example.

Russian Volgas, so we can swap ball joints, tie rods, bearings and seals," said Pastor, the head mechanic at Grancar. "The parts on the newer Volgas have newer parts, and replacements can be found easier than a 1953 Cadillac part."

Pastor was in fact working on a Cadillac when we spoke to him. It was a 1947 station wagon, and it had a total steel body, which was in very rough condition. We wondered what body company had built it.

The '47 Caddy was powered by a four-cylinder diesel engine and had disc brakes on the rear axle, drum brakes on the front. A strange mixture of parts, for sure.

NOSTALGICAR

We came across another company that provides a similar service to Grancar. But NostalgiCar was a little more contemporary, offering mechanical restoration services and installation of new drivetrain components and accessories, such as air-conditioning systems, into older cars. NostalgiCar will also rent out their cars to tourists and provide taxi services and special-event limousine services for events such as weddings.

"All the parts we install come from the States," said a man who appeared to be in charge. "We just completed a 1959 Chevy that we installed a Mercedes five-cylinder diesel engine."

9

WHEN CUBAN ★CARS★ WERE NEW

THE IMPORTATION OF NEW CARS SLOWED DRAMATICALLY AFTER THE JANUARY 1, 1959, REVOLUTION. CASTRO IMPOSED A NEARLY 200 PERCENT TAX ON LUXURY ITEMS, WHICH INCLUDED CARS, MEANING A $2,000 VEHICLE NOW COST ALMOST $6,000 TO BUY. THE TOTAL NUMBER OF NORTH AMERICAN NEW CAR SALES IN 1959 WAS 3,264, ABOUT HALF THE NUMBER SOLD THERE ONE YEAR EARLIER. US PRESIDENT DWIGHT D. EISENHOWER IMPOSED A BAN ON ALL EXPORTS TO CUBA ON OCTOBER 19, 1960, A POLICY THAT HAS BEEN IN PLACE EVER SINCE.

Cars on display at Havana's Ambar Motors GM showroom in its heyday. *Courtesy General Motors Archives*

Some retired General Motors engineer is rolling over in the grave. We saw three Corvairs in Cuba, and all of them were powered by front-engine diesels with rear-wheel drive.

Prior to the embargo, Cuba was the world's largest importer of American cars. Cuban consumers could buy new vehicles, American and European, at dealerships around Havana and throughout the country. And because Miami was so close—just a ferryboat ride away—some Cubans elected to buy their cars in Florida and bring them back. That all changed on January 1, 1959, when the Castro regime took over power.

"I used to go to Key West once a month," said our contact Quico. "The last time I was there was in 1959."

Dealerships, like many other businesses, were taken over by the government and closed because inventory was no longer available. And Cubans were no longer allowed to leave the country to make purchases.

The newest American cars seen driving on Cuban streets today, then, are 1959 models, with a few 1960 models that did squeak into the country—those actually built as early production models. During our most recent trip, we saw three Corvairs (all of which had been converted to front-engine, rear-wheel-drive configuration). Corvairs first appeared as 1960 models, so obviously these cars were shipped to Cuba early in their production cycle.

HAVANA ASSEMBLY LINES

Cuba proved to be such a healthy market for American cars that General Motors actually built a couple of subassembly plants in and around Havana. The Chevrolet plant was just a block from the Malecón.

GM brands Oldsmobile, Cadillac, Chevrolet, Pontiac, and Buick were shipped in knocked-down form from the United States to Cuba, where local laborers assembled them into running cars, using some local content. Completed cars were then shipped to dealerships around the island to be sold.

"The neighborhood around the assembly plant was called Little Detroit," said our friend Ivan. This neighborhood was also where many new car dealerships were based.

"The name of the Chevrolet assembly plant was Ambar Motors, which [was named after] the owner, Amadeo Barletta," said Eduardo Mesejo of the Depósito del Automóvil. Quico once owned and raced a 1957 Chevy that was assembled at Ambar.

"The Buick plant was called Valiant Motors, and the Pontiac plant was Villoldo Motors," he said. He also told us that in the 1920s and 1930s, Ford also had an assembly plant on the island where Model Ts and Model As were put together from knocked-down parts.

After World War II, Ford's assembly plant in Jacksonville, Florida, assembled cars for the southern US market, as well as those shipped to Cuba and other Central and South American dealers.

There is no record that European cars were ever assembled in Cuba.

ERNEST HEMINGWAY'S CHRYSLER

The famous American novelist Ernest Hemingway first visited Cuba in 1928, then again in 1933, when he was on a deep sea fishing trip.

In 1940, Hemingway purchased a modest home, called San Francisco de Paula, about nine miles from the center of Havana. To commute from this home to his favorite bars in the capital city, he purchased a Hemi-powered 1955 Chrysler New Yorker. He could be seen driving this red convertible the 12 miles from his home to the Floridita, where he would devour piña coladas and mojitos.

Word is that he would get pretty slammed on these visits.

The Floridita is very much in business today, and the bar still serves the Hemingway-approved drinks to tourists. A bronze statue of Hemingway sits on his favorite stool, which makes for a perfect

Once a new, bright-red 1955 Chrysler convertible, this car was one that novelist Ernest Hemingway once drove to cruise the streets of Havana.

RIGHT: Hemingway's Hemi-powered Chrysler is now being restored, an effort funded by actor/singer David Soul, who once played the role of Hutch on *Starsky and Hutch*.

BELOW LEFT: The correct 33-cubic-inch Hemi engine still resides in Hemingway's former Chrysler. Thankfully, this car was never converted to diesel power.

BELOW RIGHT: If this VIN could talk, imagine the stories it could tell about its former famous owner's Cuban escapades, celebrities that may have ridden in the car, etc.

BOTTOM: Hemingway rented this sweet villa from when he summered in Cuba in the 1950s until he died in 1961. The house has been restored and is open as a museum.

"selfie" photo op for tourists. It wouldn't take much to imagine the red convertible parked on the curb while the slightly looped author held court there.

The San Francisco de Paula home is now the Ernest Hemingway Museum. His boat, *Pilar*, is on display—as is the swimming pool, where he used to skinny-dip with Ava Gardner. (He did live big!) Photos of Hemingway and Castro are displayed around the pristine home.

Hemingway's old Chrysler is being restored, funded by actor and singer David Soul. Soul is best known for his role as Detective "Hutch" on the television program *Starsky and Hutch*. He has taken a real interest in Hemingway, but especially his Chrysler, which apparently will be featured in a television special about both Hemingway and his car.

TOP RIGHT: The authors frequented the Floridita during their stay, "strictly for research purposes." Here co-author Bill Warner spends time with his friend Ernie.

RIGHT: Hemingway used to park his convertible on the curb here in front of the Floridita, his favorite watering hole.

BELOW: The study where Hemingway may have written some of his novels.

BELOW RIGHT: Inside the Floridita, which boasts being "the Cradle of the Daiquiri." The authors of this book can verify that the mojitos and piña coladas are exceptional as well.

The sky, the ocean, the fence posts, and the landscape provide a lovely color palate to complement this mint-green 1950 Chevy. *Merten Snijders/ Getty Images*

HAVANA'S MEGA-DEALER

As previously mentioned, Ambar Motors (founded in 1948) was owned by Amadeo Barletta, the business name being made of the first letters of his first and last names. Barletta was born in Italy in 1894 but spent his youth in Puerto Rico. As a twenty-six-year-old, he opened the first Chevy dealership in the Dominican Republic in 1920.

In 1939, Barletta was named by Italy's Benito Mussolini as the ambassador to Cuba. Because Italy and Cuba were not allies, Barletta was expelled from Cuba at the start of World War II.

After the war, however, Barletta came back to Cuba and opened up his dealership in Havana

Ambar Motors had a beautiful showroom that displayed Cadillacs, Oldsmobiles, and other GM products. Looking at these Caddys and Oldsmobiles made us wonder whether, sixty years later, we had possibly seen some of the exact same cars driving on Havana streets. *Courtesy General Motors Archives*

The same building that once housed an Ambar Motors dealership, assembly plant, and parts warehouse today has apartments on the upper stories and retail stores on the street level.

selling Chevrolets, Oldsmobiles, and Cadillacs, as well as Chevy trucks and GM buses. By 1945, Ambar operated more than thirty GM dealerships and sub-dealerships around the country, including ten in Havana alone. The business occupied a modernistic building at the corner of the Malecón and La Rampa, Havana's main east-west street. The glass showroom displayed cars along two blocks in central Havana. By 1951, Ambar Motors employed more than two hundred employees and sold more than seven thousand vehicles annually.

After the revolution, Barletta saw the writing on the wall and realized that his income was in jeopardy, so he left Cuba and moved to the Dominican Republic to run the dealership he began there decades earlier.

Interestingly, for more than twenty years, Ambar Motors has operated three large used-car dealerships in South Florida.

NOT A DRIVER'S PARADISE

Not surprisingly, with so many cars on the road, navigating Havana's streets and finding a parking space takes patience. A columnist in the 1950s wrote, "Our beautiful city is an immense parking garage, where parking and driving means resigned patience and finely honed skills, now that our streets and avenues are congested with automobiles, buses, and trucks, without the least effort being made to remedy the situation."

From what we've seen on our two trips to Cuba over the past ten years, not much has changed in road management or congestion in the ensuing half century.

Cubans who desired to buy a new car in the 1950s often had to finance their new asset. But interest rates added roughly 37 percent to the cost of a new car, meaning a car with a sticker price of US$1,546 would actually cost $3,275 when finance charges were included.

In 1959, only 3,264 cars were imported from the United States to Cuba, roughly half the number from the previous year. A late shipment that year of a few Oldsmobiles and Chevys made it into the country before the gates closed.

Despite the lack of cars from America's "big three," however, Cuba hosted an International Auto Show in Havana in late 1959. One of the more interesting vehicles that participated was a "flying car" that was manufactured in Massachusetts, which was driven by the builder from the plant to Key West, Florida, then flown the 90 miles to Havana. Great promotion. An article about the journey said the flying car achieved elevation of 12,000 feet and could reach a top air speed of one hundred miles per hour.

Plans for another show were made for 1960, touting the benefits of that year's new model features, but that show never happened. Cuban residents were about to start feeling the negative effects of their revolution, and those "New for 1960" features wouldn't be seen in 1960, or even in 2015.

As of our 2015 trip to Cuba, the original Ambar Motors building was still standing, but it now houses the Ministry of Foreign Trade, retail stores, and apartments.

CHEVY VS. FORD

We noticed as we drove throughout the city and the country that 1955, 1956, and 1957 Chevys were more common than any other vintage car brand. Was it our imagination?

No. The Ambar assembly line and Cuban GM dealerships built and sold more Chevys during the mid-1950s than any other brand. The abundance of "Tri-Five" Chevys in the 1950s is still reflected today at nearly every intersection.

NEW CARS NOW

The streets of Cuba are not only populated with old American cars— there are some new, or at least newer, cars as well. In 2011, President Raúl Castro made it legal for Cubans to buy and sell new and used cars for the first time since 1959.

Part of the economic reforms Raúl has rolled out since taking over as president of Cuba from his brother, Fidel, who stepped down in 2008, the regulations allowed for the legal "transfer of ownership of vehicles for purchase, sale, or donation among Cubans living on the island or foreigners who are residents of Cuba."

We saw a couple of new car dealerships during our visit, but they were not very crowded. According to our translator, new car purchases might now be legal, but they are still unaffordable for 99 percent of the population.

"When a 15,000 CUC Chinese car costs 250,000 CUCs, nobody can afford to buy one," he said.

Our translator told us that Cuban cultural figures—athletes, musicians, and artists—have always been able to buy new cars at much friendlier rates than average citizens.

Bougainvillea grows like a weed and blooms year round all over Cuba. *Buena Vista Images/Getty Images*

We saw this handsome 1958 Chevrolet Impala convertible along the docks of Havana.

10
DRIVING AROUND THE ★ ISLAND TODAY

THE FIRST TIME WE VISITED CUBA, WE HIRED BOTH A TOUR GUIDE AND A DRIVER WITH A VAN. THIS GAVE US THE OPPORTUNITY TO BE TOURISTS AND LOOK AT ALL THE OLD CARS INSTEAD OF WATCHING OUT FOR TRAFFIC. THE VAN WAS A PEUGEOT, AND IT HAD AIR CONDITIONING, SO IT WAS A PLEASANT RIDE FOR THE WEEK WE VISITED.

ON OUR MOST RECENT TRIP, WE RENTED A CAR—A CHINESE GEELY EMGRAND—FROM CUBACAR, ONE OF THE TWO GOVERNMENT-OWNED RENTAL AGENCIES. THE RENTAL EXPERIENCE WAS NOT IDEAL; WE SAT IN FRONT OF A RENTAL

An eclectic mixture of Soviet and American vehicles, this is the daily traffic jam that surrounds Havana's city center. *Fotografia Inc./Getty Images*

ABOVE: Looking sparkling and clean from across the bay, the city's sixty-year-old infrastructure is clearly in need of repairs and rebuilding when viewed up close.

OPPOSITE: Not much has changed in sixty years. Making their way through the center of Havana are this 1956 Chevy, 1957 Ford wagon, and 1955 Ford sedan.

counter in a hot, humid, and crowded lobby along with a dozen or so other tourists, waiting for cars to be returned. Even though we had reservations, nobody could confirm whether we would be able to secure a car within the next several hours. Or the next several days.

Luckily, we were only there a short time before a friend of ours came and arranged for us to get the next available car. (Part of that underground economy.) We felt bad for the other folks in line, some of whom had been waiting for six hours! One recently married couple needed to rent their car so they could drive to their honeymoon resort, which was a couple hours down the coast.

The rental rate for the Geely was CUC$120 per day (about US$120), and with fuel our five-day stay cost about CUC$900. Our car was a smaller Toyota Corolla–sized model, as opposed to the

ABOVE: Rarely do new cars, such as this snazzy Peugeot sport coupe, appear in Cuba. Obviously this belongs to a wealthy musician or athlete—who get large salaries and preferential treatment.

BELOW: Youth at speed! No matter what continent or culture, young people love to live life in the fast lane.

larger Geely, which resembles a Cadillac ATS—right down to the logo on the grille. Ours was a front-wheel-drive, four-cylinder, five-speed, four-door sedan. It was fine and had good air conditioning, which was a blessing in July when temperatures hit a hundred degrees with high humidity.

The car felt tight when we picked it up because it was nearly new. It was not quite as tight when we returned it five days later; we had nailed a dozen major potholes, and metallic sounds were coming from the suspension.

In our defense, some of the potholes are so deep that a Baja racer or a Humvee would barely be able to navigate those streets without getting damaged. It makes you wonder how the half-century-old cars have lasted as long as this, having had to drive through these pitted streets day after day, year after year, decade after decade.

We wondered: would cars like our rental Geely still be on the road in fifty years, in 2065? We doubted it. These cars are "throwaways"—cars that are cheap to build and operate but have short lifespans. Nothing like the iron monsters that Detroit pumped out in the 1950s.

SPEEDING

Our friend Eduardo told us to watch our speed. The top speed limit in Havana's city limits is 80 kilometers per hour (50 miles per hour). Speed limits in the country, though, can go as high as 120 kilometers per hour.

One day we took a drive along the coast to do a little sightseeing. The day was beautiful, and it was easy to forget the slow posted speed limit because of the beautiful scenery on all sides—ocean on the left, mountains on the right—and the roads were fairly smooth. Suddenly a police officer stepped out in front of our car and pointed us to the side of the road. He walked over to our car and pointed to his radar gun. We had been traveling at 73 kilometers per hour in a 60-kilometer-per-hour zone.

Not knowing any English, he told us we could go. Nice guy.

PUNTE CONTROLE

Punte controle are police checkpoints that are set up along most country roads. They can be radar traps or simply locations for police to check credentials.

Interestingly, there is no such thing as car insurance for citizens in Cuba. However, tourists who rent cars should purchase the optional insurance policy, which often costs more than the actual rental costs.

CAR PARKERS

One local custom that visitors must become comfortable with when motoring around Cuba is the regular interaction with "parkers." Parkers are people who must be paid to "watch your car" and are stationed outside nearly every grocery store, hotel, and restaurant in the country. These red-vested people make their living by collecting money from motorists, usually CUC$1, to watch cars until the owners come out of the store or restaurant.

Besides being a highly boring job, there is no evidence that these parkers have ever actually prevented anything from happening to the cars they watch.

Most of the vehicles darting around Havana's city center are hauling ass. This driver was content with simply hauling ice.

LEFT: Murals by artist Salvador Gonzalez on Havana's street of Callejón de Hamel. *Kike Calvo/Getty Images*

ABOVE AND BELOW: This public market offers local artwork and souvenirs of Cuba including, cigars, papier-mâché models, and locally made trinkets.

CROSS-COUNTRY (CUBA)

Tom could not make the trek to Cuba during a trip I took in 2011, so my friends Mike and Cynthia Sierra, both of Cuban descent and fluent in Cuban Spanish, met me in Miami for the forty-five-minute flight to Havana.

Our goal was to visit the car museum in Santiago de Cuba, about 600 miles east of Havana in the Oriente Province, and check out a late Silver Ghost on display at a local college in Camagüey en route. Unfortunately, when we got to the school, it was a holiday and the school was closed—so we were off to Santiago.

The distance from Havana to Santiago de Cuba is 870 kilometers (550 miles), and being a naïve American who likes to crank out 600 to 700 miles a day, I thought the trip looked like a piece of cake. Cuba's best highway is the four-lane C1, and with little or no traffic, save for trucks and buses, it appeared to be a no-brainer . . . not.

Leaving Havana at 8:30 a.m. in our rented diesel van, we headed east. I was in the driver's seat, and with the light traffic and a speed limit of 100 kilometers per hour, I was bored to death, so I rested my elbow on the windowsill and propped up my head. Next thing I knew, I was being pulled over by a motorcycle cop. I wasn't speeding—well, maybe a little—but he was convinced that I had been talking on a cell phone while driving, which in Cuba is a no-no.

Once it was determined that I was just bored, we were free to proceed.

The C1 does not run the full length of the island (which is 750 miles long and 40 miles wide), and once on the back roads, you will find that road signs are as lacking as are centerlines. A wide variety of highway flotsam and jetsam are liable to be around the next curve. That can include dogs, oxen, goats, cows, sheep, people on bikes, wheelchairs, motor scooters, and most anything else with wheels. Although we did not arrive in Santiago de Cuba until about 9:00 p.m., I do *not* advise driving at night in Cuba or in the rain, which is particularly dangerous.

Having learned our lesson trying to blast across the country in one day, we decided to make our return trip in two. En route back to Havana, we stayed at the beautiful Meliá Cayo Santa María Resort. The quality of the construction of the resort was

Mike Sierra is a successful lawyer and car collector in Ybor City, near Tampa, Florida, whose grandparents emigrated from Cuba to the United States one hundred years ago. Mike is also a collector of pre-1914 Rolls-Royce Silver Ghosts, owning six of them.

pretty bad, but the beach was fabulous, with the bougainvillea in full bloom and the food plentiful, if somewhat bland. To get to the resort, one has to take a 40-kilometer causeway to the remote island. The Cuban government has suspected its people of using the island as a jumping-off point for defecting, so we had to show our passports to reach the hotel.

All over Cuba, we noticed a complete lack of boats that could be used to reach the Florida Keys.

Returning to Havana on the north coast allowed us to visit Varadero, Cuba's premier resort area. Since our first visit, the resort has exploded with developments primarily for tourists.

When leaving Varadero, we faced four black BMW 7 Series sedans with flashing blue and red lights in a V formation, one in the lead, one behind, and two flanking the center car. We were told that it was most likely Raúl Castro on his way to his estate at the end of the peninsula. Even the communist leaders enjoy the trappings of success.

One surprise on our return trip was driving through Cuba's oil fields . . . yes, Cuba has oil, but not much, and what they do have is high in sulfur content, we were told. Cuba gets most of its oil from Venezuela, but with tumbling oil prices and the collapsing Venezuelan economy, Cuba is in a difficult position.

We did see huge, modern oil rigs flying Chinese flags. The Chinese are anxious to assist the Cubans in developing their oil assets or at least drill in the Straits of Florida, where the United States is reluctant to drill. At the time of this writing, drilling for new oil is not a wise economic move, what with the glut on the market.

For anyone wishing to tour Cuba on their own, I highly recommend buying a copy of the *DK Eyewitness Travel Guide: Cuba*. It is superb.

—Bill Warner

ABOVE: Not too many miles from downtown Havana, the beauty of rural Cuba is obvious. Virtually all land outside of the cities is used for agriculture.

BELOW: Most tourists are surprised to learn that areas of Cuba are quite mountainous. This spectacular bridge connects Havana with the Varadero resort.

11

TWO ★ AUTO ★ MUSEUMS

C UBA'S STREETS ARE LIKE A LIVING MUSEUM WITH SIXTY-PLUS-YEAR-OLD CARS SCOOTING BACK AND FORTH IN A NEVER-ENDING METALLIC SYMPHONY. BUT BECAUSE THE COUNTRY RESPECTS ITS HISTORY, AND HAS NUMEROUS MUSEUMS THAT DISPLAY EVERYTHING FROM REVOLUTIONARY WAR RELICS TO MODERN ART, IT IS NOT SURPRISING THAT THERE ARE ALSO TWO AUTO MUSEUMS, SEPARATED BY ABOUT 600 MILES.

DEPÓSITO DEL AUTOMÓVIL

Within two hours of touching down at the Havana airport during our first trip to Cuba in 2009, we visited the Depósito del Automóvil, Havana's antique car museum. We thought this would be the ideal place to begin our search for old

This 1926 Rolls-Royce sports French bodywork by Letourneur et Marchand. It was kept in storage after the revolution and presented to the museum when it opened in 1980.

This photo of the Havana auto museum was taken during our first trip to Cuba. When a portion of the building collapsed and destroyed some of the cars, it was moved to another location in the same historic neighborhood.

cars, plus director Eduardo Mesejo Maestre was our only English-speaking contact on the island until we connected with our tour guide, Abel.

We were naïve during that first trip, thinking we could actually "sneak" around the capital and find a warehouse that might actually contain Fidel Castro's own cars—in other words, explore "Castro's garage." But once we saw the guards with machine guns around the city, and heard the stories about foreigners who were sitting in prison because they tried to explore around the executive mansion, we decided that was not such a good idea. So the museum would have to suffice.

"Fidel used to drive Oldsmobiles in 1957 and '58," said Eduardo. "And he drove Soviet cars, including Soviet Jeeps, after the revolution. But Fidel is not a car enthusiast. He doesn't care about cars."

Eduardo did tell us that current Cuban president Raúl Castro favors BMWs, though.

The Depósito del Automóvil is humble when compared to most antique car museums in America. But even though the cars are somewhat underwhelming, some have interesting histories. Admission to the museum, which opened in 1980, costs CUC$1, and children are free. Visitors are treated to an inventory of about forty cars, trucks, and motorcycles.

The museum is located in the historic district of Havana, but it changed locations between our first and most recent trips because the original building's roof collapsed.

"The humidity and lack of maintenance caused the timbers to rot and the roof to collapse," said Eduardo. Several of the cars, including a couple of Model A Fords, received body damage ranging from minor dings to total demolition. The museum is now located in an attractive waterside building just a couple blocks from the original location.

This 1915 Mack truck, a Senior model, was in use until 1970, still giving its owner reliable service at fifty-five years old.

Eduardo Mesejo is proud of the progress his museum staff is making on the country's oldest vehicle, a 1905 Cadillac.

The Depósito's inventory includes two cars that were instrumental in the 1959 revolution: the green 1960 Chevrolet Bel Air driven by Castro coconspirator Che Guevara and the 1959 Oldsmobile Rocket 88 of Camilo Cienfuegos. Some of the other notable cars in the museum include:

ROLLS-ROYCE PHANTOM

The star of the collection is the 1926 Rolls-Royce Phantom, with the body fabricated by Letourneur et Marchand of France. Eduardo told us that this car was found abandoned after the revolution and kept safe by the government until the museum opened in 1980.

The Rolls is not in pristine condition, as you would imagine a similar car to look in the States. It is simply a used, unrestored car that is given a sponge bath every day to remove the caustic dust caused by the many building renovations occurring in the area.

BRASS-ERA CADDY

The other car that Eduardo is particularly excited about is the 1905 Cadillac, which was apparently in continuous use on Cuban roads until forty years ago. It was one of the first cars to be brought into the museum.

"It was an everyday car," said Eduardo. "It would drive around the Havana streets until the 1970s." He also told us in 2009 that the Cadillac was scheduled to undergo a complete and thorough restoration.

"The previous owner of the Cadillac received a new Russian Lada in exchange for his old car. This will be the first professional restoration of a classic car in Cuban history. We received much of the technical information from car collectors in the Philadelphia area. The engineering knowledge of this car was very important to have before we begin restoration," he said. Eduardo, who has a mechanical engineering degree and is working on his doctorate, takes a very academic approach to historic vehicles.

"When verifying an historic car, first deny, then investigate, third, believe."

The Cadillac's chassis and suspension have been sandblasted and epoxy painted, and a local woodworker has been contracted to rebuild the four-seater body. But not much work had progressed between our 2009 and 2015 visits to the museum, likely due to a complete lack of a budget.

FANGIO'S MASER

Probably the most intriguing car in the Depósito is not a car at all but a prop.

Parked front and center on the museum floor is what appears to be a bright blue Maserati. It appears, in fact, to be the racer that five-time

world champion Juan Manuel Fangio drove in the 1957 Grand Prix.

It is not a real car, however. It is a reproduction shell that resembles Fangio's Maserati. It was built by an Argentine film company for a movie they were producing about the great driver.

"It is made of fiberglass," said Eduardo. "Many people who come to the museum see it from a distance and don't know it isn't real. We actually painted it in the street with a sponge. Part of the suspension is from a Citroën; it has a plywood chassis and homemade wire wheels.

"It looks correct when it's in the background."

CHAIN-DRIVE MACK

Another curious vehicle is the 1915 Mack Senior dump truck, which was in constant use until 1970. It has a fresh coat of paint (no doubt applied by sponge) and looks impressive and purposeful.

From a distance, this Maserati 300S gets enthusiasts excited as they walk into the museum, but in fact it is a fiberglass-and-plywood movie prop that was donated to the museum after its movie career was over.

Our tour guide had one of the few 1955 Chevys with not only an original "stovebolt" six but also air conditioning—a rare option in Cuba.

ECLECTIC ASSORTMENT

The museum's inventory includes other vehicles that wouldn't necessarily increase the blood pressure of an American enthusiast. Some of those (with comments by Eduardo) include:

1969 ALFA ROMEO SPIDER

Eduardo has known of this car since it was new. "My father wouldn't let me get any closer than one meter away, which is very hard for a young boy. Many years later, the car came to the museum and I was finally able to touch it. I sat in the car for one hour. It is the love of my life."

1953 DODGE

The dark-brown sedan has special meaning for Eduardo. "That car was my father's. I inherited it and learned to drive in that car. It never let our family down."

HIDDEN FIAT

"The car was hidden behind a wall for fifty years. The owner was a woman whose father was an important general in the 1800s. During one of our tyrannies, she decided to have the car hidden behind a wall in her mansion."

EARLY 1980s CHEVY IMPALA

What? How did this monument of capitalism wind up in Cuba? "Ambassadors often gave cars as gifts to Castro. Those cars were stored in the Central

The museum in Santiago de Cuba is housed in an open shed and contains a mixture of old cars, trucks, and tractors.

Communist Committee warehouse. Either that or ambassadors just left their official or personal cars to the government when they left Cuba, and they were given to us."

PARQUE BACONAO

After seeing the Depósito del Automóvil, we set off for Santiago de Cuba to find the museum located in a local park there. Upon arrival, we were met by the curator, who at one time had worked on the Russian Lada Rally team.

The "museum" was essentially an open L-shaped shed in the Parque Baconao and includes a selection of some fairly shabby cars, mostly brush painted, some missing glass backlights or

ABOVE: Two elegant cars from the past--a 1954 Buick Skylark (left) and a 1948 Mercury convertible—on display at the Santiago de Cuba museum.

BELOW: The only car that was actually designed and built in Cuba—the Maya. About the size of a King Midget, it represents Communism at its finest in the Santiago de Cuba Museum.

side windows, and all on jack stands. Two of the rarest or most interesting are a 1954 Buick Skylark and a 1957 Cadillac Eldorado Coupe de Ville.

Was it worth the drive? To see the museum, no, but to see the "real" Cuba, yes. The Santiago de Cuba area is quite nice, and the hotel where we stayed—the Meliá Santiago de Cuba—was very nice, though dated, like a 1960s Miami hotel. We also found a rare early Ford-powered racer owned by a Cuban exile in Miami and a 1949 Buick Super Convertible during our travels in the city.

A trip to Santiago de Cuba would not be complete without visiting the Castillo del Morro, a fortress guarding the entrance of the Bay of Santiago, that was built between 1638 and 1700. The view is spectacular, and the fort well maintained by the state.

Santiago de Cuba is a very nice city, and we wish we'd had more time to explore the area.

This Karmann Ghia, on display at the Santiago de Cuba Museum, is certainly newer than 1959, when the US embargo began. But Germany did not initiate an embargo, so later-model European cars were still available to those who could afford them.

12
YOU CAN'T BRING ★ THEM HOME!

SO MANY CAR ENTHUSIASTS IN THE STATES CLAIM THAT AS SOON AS THE CUBAN/AMERICAN EMBARGO IS OVER, THEY'LL GO DOWN THERE AND BUY UP ALL THE OLD CARS. NOT LIKELY.

FIRST OF ALL, THESE CARS ARE VALUED BY CUBA AS TREASURES OF THE STATE, AND IT IS ILLEGAL AND VERY NEARLY IMPOSSIBLE TO SEND A CAR OUT OF THE COUNTRY EXCEPT IN THE MOST UNUSUAL CIRCUMSTANCES.

SECOND, YOU WOULDN'T REALLY WANT ONE. THE ROUGH CONDITION OF THESE CARS WOULD NOT MAKE THEM VERY DESIRABLE IN THE UNITED STATES, OR ANYWHERE ELSE. CARS IN MUCH BETTER CONDITION CAN BE PURCHASED HERE IN THE STATES, AND THE PURCHASER

This Chevy Deluxe four-door is an example of one the better early 1950s cars on the island. *lazyllama/Shutterstock*

ABOVE: No, you can't bring this Pontiac back to the States, but would you really want to? For every "pretty" car seen in Cuba, twenty more can be seen in this condition.

OPPOSITE RIGHT: A car like this late-1940s Chevy sedan would have minimal investment value in the United States, but in Cuba, it is somebody's pride and joy. It's probably better just to leave it there.

can be more confident that Russian parts were not part of the package. Not so in Cuba, where parts from any car, regardless of vintage or origin, can be used in the repair of any other car.

Besides condition, value comes into the equation. Go to Craigslist, eBay, or *Hemmings Motor News* and you'll find cars in the United States in better condition for half the price the Cubans would be asking for their cars.

Finally, it is difficult to determine just who has legal claim to many of the cars. As in the case of the BMW 507 mentioned earlier (see page 121), courts may deem the car you squired out of Cuba stolen property and require you to forfeit your claim to it.

LEAVING ON A JET PLANE

The day we left Cuba, July 20, 2015, was the day the US embassy was reopened for the first time since 1961. As we drove our Geely rental car toward the airport, crowds were gathering and television cameras were in place for the big news conference that was scheduled to take place in just a couple hours.

Clearly, we were eyewitnesses to changes in the Cuban-American relationship. After fifty years of a US trade embargo, the walls were rapidly coming down.

Within the span of time that this manuscript was being written, the US embassy resumed operating with a full staff, travel restrictions were gradually eased, discussions were being held to begin cell phone and ATM services, and President Barack Obama made his historic visit to the country.

What does all this mean for car guys?

That potentially an exchange of parts and information can flow between the two countries without roadblocks. That perhaps cars will be sold between the two countries in both directions. And that citizens of both nations can participate in races, shows, and other automotive events without regard to borders.

We need some car-guy diplomacy between Cuba and the United States, just like it used to be.

"I can only hope that things will get better between our two countries," said our friend Quico as we were leaving. It is a sentiment shared by enthusiasts on both sides of the border.

GETTING CARS IN AND OUT OF CUBA

Because our friend Ivan is both a lawyer and car collector, we asked him what hurdles would need to be crossed to import or export a car into or out of Cuba.

"If you wanted to buy a car in Cuba and export it, that is not possible right now," he said. "Some people have done it, but it is done illegally. Some people are buying cars in Cuba now and storing them in the country until the gates open. Then they plan to ship them home.

"You can legally export a car from Cuba if, one, you are a Cuban citizen who legally owns property outside of the country, and with [a guarantee to] the government that you will ship it back to Cuba again; or, two, with government approval, you can ship a vintage car overseas for the purpose of restoration if that quality of restoration is not possible in Cuba."

Ivan added this about proof of ownership: "Ownership equals possession of the property for twenty years or more. Then any previous owners have no claim to the car."

That of course could theoretically be challenged in the future.

TOP: Sadly, the once-mighty American brands of Cadillac, Oldsmobile, Ford, and this Buick, have been reduced to hastily repaired taxis. But amazingly, they are still on the road.

FINAL THOUGHTS

★

Cuba observers are experiencing history in the making. During the spring of 2016, US Secretary of Transportation Anthony Foxx traveled to Havana and negotiated an agreement with the Cuban government for as many as one hundred commercial flights per day from the United States to Cuba, and President Obama became the first sitting US president to visit the island nation since Calvin Coolidge in 1928.

Policies are certainly changing quickly.

Bill and I traveled to Cuba on a cultural exchange visa, but like most enthusiasts, we were curious to see if cars could be purchased, then sold back in the States for profit. But as you read, 99.9 percent of the cars are not worth bringing back. Except for the odd Porsche Carrera or Mercedes 300SL, most of the cars we saw are not worthy of the 90-mile trip north.

But the great news is for Cuban motorists who have been bandaging these cars together with junk parts for more than half a century.

When relations resume between our two countries, Cubans will finally be able to obtain the parts and tools they need to correctly repair their

cars for the first time since 1959. And they might even have the opportunity to buy newer cars with features that the rest of us take for granted, such as air conditioning.

When that wall comes down, maybe the big winners will be those millions of Cuban citizens who have suffered under a failed government for so many years.

That's probably the best outcome of all.

—TOM COTTER

People often ask me if Cuba will change or how will Cuba change. Will Cuba change? Absolutely! It has to, as Communism (or socialism . . . you choose) has devastated the country, and the rest of the world has left it behind in quality of life, education, productivity, and the freedom to be self-sufficient. What will drive the change? I feel the Internet will have as big an impact as anything. Cubans are intelligent and resourceful and, providing they embrace a form of capitalism, they will succeed. As we have mentioned elsewhere in this book, there is a pent-up desire to improve their lot. As for the pre-1960s cars, as soon as Cubans can earn more money than the stipend the government gives them, they will be buying newer, more modern cars. It could very well be that good used cars will be exported from the United States to address the needs of the Cuban people. If—and that is a big "if"—they can develop their oil resources, it could be a game changer. I've enjoyed my trips to Cuba as well as my relationships with the members of the car culture there. Things will change—the only question I ask myself is how long will it take and over what period of time ?

—BILL WARNER

BIBLIOGRAPHY

Cotter, Tom. "Cuba's Time Capsule." *New York Times*, June 3, 2010.

Eisenstein, Paul A. "Is Cuba a Hidden Trove of Classic Cars?" The Detroit Bureau, January 30, 2015. www.thedetroitbureau.com

Finn, Joel E. *Caribbean Capers*. Boston: Racemaker Press, 2010.

Gross, Ken. "Rolling Ghosts." *Autoweek*, May 11, 2015.

LeBlanc, Jean-Pierre. "Cuba: A Living Car Museum." *Buick Bugle*, May 2011.

Lentinello, Richard. *Hemming's Daily*, March 23, 2006; May 25, 2006; November 9, 2006.

Navarro, Mireya. "Cuban Wizardry Keep Tailfins from Drooping." *New York Times*, June 5, 2002.

Schweid, Richard. *Che's Chevrolet, Castro's Oldsmobile*. Chapel Hill: University of North Carolina Press, 2004.

Wheeler, William. "Engine Trouble." *Playboy*, March 2015.

"Today I offer the Cuban people a hundred thousand '94 Ford Explorers for one '57 Chevy." *Larry Trepel*

INDEX

Longitude du Mér.

294   295   296   297   298

25

24

23

22

21

20

19

Pte de Janche

Isles Bimi

les Martirs

les Tortues Seches

DÉTROIT DE FLORIDE

Laxa ⊙

Bahia Honda

Maciel

LA HAVANNE

Pte d'Hicaque

Rte de Matanzas

Basses et Cayes de Ste Isabelle

Bte de la Pon

Fr Arostegas   Fr Atur.es

Tete du Dauphin

El Morro

el Havana

Fr Arostegas

Guanabacoa

Jaruco

Paan de Matanzas

Fort

Matanzas

Santiago de la Vega

M. de Haronques

M. de Carahatas

Sr Felice

LOS

Villa Clara

Reni

Batahano

S. Felipe

Limones Grandes

Camarones

LLANOS

Mte de Rio Puerco

San Felipe

Macurites

B de Xaguas

Cap St Antoine

la Grosse Pte

Cte corientes

R. de Cortés

la Trinidad

Golfe de Xaguas

ISLE DE PINOS

les Jardins

L'ISLE DE CUBA.
Par
M. Bonne Ingénieur-Hydrographe
de la Marine.

Lieues d'Espagne de 17½ au Degré.

5   10   15   20   25   30   35

Lieues legales de Castille de 26½ au Degré.

5   10   20   30   40   50   53

Cayman Brac

Petit Cayman

Grand Cayman

86   85   84   83   82

Longitude du